THOUGHTS

ON THE

IMPORTANCE

OF THE

MANNERS OF THE GREAT

TO

GENERAL SOCIETY.

AND AN ESTIMATE

OF THE RELIGION

OF THE

FASHIONABLE WORLD.

BY HANNAH MORE.

A NEW EDITION.

London:

PRINTED FOR T. CADELL AND W. DAVIES, STRAND.

1809.

PREFACE.

It has often occurred to the Author, that it would furnish a fair subject for discussion, to determine whether it argues more vanity when a writer prefixes his name to his book, or when he publishes without it;—whether it implies more self-sufficiency to suppose that his name is of so much value as to attract readers to his work, or to trust so confidently to the merit of the

a

work itself, as to depend on its unassisted strength for making its own
way.—In short, whether the presump-
tion be greater in thinking better of
himself, or of his book; and how the
proportion of good opinion can be
settled or separated.

This is a dilemma in which the writer
of these pages has not seldom been
involved, having not unfrequently
indulged her vanity, or her humility,
whichever it may be called, under both
shapes, without being able to ascertain
on which side the real difference lies.
Nor can she decide which principle
predominated in risking these two little

works anonymously, near twenty years
ago, or in afterwards publishing them,
with a name which she had little right
to expect could confer importance on
any performance.

There is, however, one decided advantage which belongs to the anony-
mous writer. He is not restrained
from the strongest reprehension, and
most pointed censure, of existing errors,
by the conscious apprehension that his
own faults may be brought forward.
He is under no fear that his negligences
will be opposed to his reproofs. He is
not deterred from expatiating on the
deficiencies of others, by the fear that

the reader may confront his life with his arguments.

Being now called upon by her Book-sellers to unite these separate pieces into one volume, the Author cannot neglect so fair an occasion of expressing her gratitude for the very favourable reception which they severally expe-rienced in their unacknowledged state, seven large editions of the first of these pieces having been called for in the course of a few months, and the whole third impression having been sold on the morning it was published, serve, among repeated instances of general favour, to increase her regret that the merit of her writings have not borne more proportion to the indulgence with which they have been received.

May she venture to observe, without incurring the charge of over-rating her slight performances, that there is a point of view in which this success reflects no discredit on the public opinion? For, does it not evince that where the obvious aim of a writer is to promote the interests of Christian morals, the effort, however feeble, will be candidly accepted; nor will the deficiencies of the composition be allowed to defeat the honesty of the intention.

The lapse of years since the first

appearance of these two small pieces,
has only served to strengthen the conviction that such topics as they embrace, cannot be pressed too closely, or
too frequently, though they may be
pressed far more ably, on the attention
of the great and the gay,—on the consciences of the busy and the opulent.

The awful and unparalleled public
events which have occurred since these
"Thoughts on the Manners of the Great,"
" and this Estimate of the Religion of
the Fashionable," were first addressed to
them, seem to furnish no new reason
why the standard of Religion which
these Tracts presumed to hold up should
be lowered, while the strictness of practice

which they ventured to suggest, should
be relaxed. Have we beheld any
such additional instances of the sta-
bility of greatness, as teach us that
it is become more safe than formerly to build on the certainty of
earthly prosperity? Have we seen any
such new evidences of the permanency
of human grandeur, as to induce us, by
any fresh conviction of its security, to
an increased neglect of the things
which are eternal?

So far from it, will even the most
careless observer refuse to acknowledge,
that if ever there was a period in which
the demand for elevating the tone of

Christianity, principle, and correct conduct was more imperious than another, that period is the present?

If this country, which God has signally distinguished, by preserving it from the almost universal wreck of Empire—which God has signally honoured by rendering it the exclusive Asylum for the persecuted, the plundered, and the destitute of all Europe, the sole refuge of a distracted world;— if this country has been singled out from among the nations of the earth, by such pre-eminent favour, should not such a country be anxiously desirous to render itself more worthy of its high destination, in having been preserved itself, and appointed the preserver of others? As it would on the one hand be unreasonable to plead our trials and difficulties as apology for relaxing our moral discipline, it would be unfair in the other, to produce it as a motive for diminishing our gratitude. Are we not then loudly called upon to acknowledge the mercy of these providential distinctions, by exhibiting in our improved practice *that* consistency which is the life and spirit, as well as the criterion of real goodness.

While England is establishing a splendid reputation abroad, by every act of wise and vigorous resistance to the oppressor of mankind, and by every instance of disinterested liberality to the oppressed, should she not be equally anxious to establish a solid glory at home, by sedulously labouring to raise the depressed tone of virtuous practice? Should she not be jealous to evince, that her unexampled generosity to strangers is stimulated by the only pure and noble principle of action? And will not this be most unequivocally demonstrated by the only infallible test, a proportionable attention to domestic religion?

While Great Britain is exhibiting a glorious energy in the cause of a nation,

brave and generous like herself, yet
professing an erroneous worship, let
her convince that nation that she is
actuated in assisting her, by the spirit
of a religion that is indeed *reformed ;*
a religion which having the love of
God for its motive, has consequently
for its end, charity to mankind without
distinction of country or of religion.

We are become conspicuous like a
city set on a hill. We are " the observed of all observers." While the eyes of
the whole world are fixed upon us, let
the whole world perceive that our active
services, our warm benevolence to our
suffering fellow-creatures, flow from the

only principle which can sanctify right
conduct, from the only source which can
recommend it to the favour of God,
Let us prove to them that the religion
of the reformation is not a mere term, a
nominal distinction, but an improved
practical principle, discovering its superiority by its effects. Let us not let slip
the present sublime occasion of illus-
trating the faith which we profess, by a
conduct not derogatory to that high profession.

While we cannot too highly value
ourselves on being Britons, let us never
forget that we must not rest in it as a

mere local distinction.—While we justly triumph in our unparalleled constitution, let us remember that it is not a mere political distinction, glorious as that is, which must finally save us. Let us be persuaded that the paramount superiority of our happy country will consist in acting up to the spirit of that religion which it professes.—That it is not enough that its spirit is transfused into our laws—it is not enough even that it is taught in its public worship, and secured in its invaluable establishment, but that, if it would operate effectually, it must operate individually; if it would operate on the people, it must

operate on their superiors, it must be
received into the heart, and exhibited
in the life of the rich and the great.
By adopting this measure, and only by
adopting it, can Christianity be rescued
from the anomaly with which its enemies have stigmatized it, that the practice of Christians does not more uniformly exemplify the doctrines of its
Author.

Thanks to the English spirit, we want
at this moment of peril, no Tyrtœus to
awake our valour, for it never slumbers.
But we want " the warning voice of
him who saw the Apocalypse" to rouse

us from our *moral* slumber. We want
not to be stimulated to public spirit, but
to individual virtue: not to exertion for
others, but to vigilance over ourselves;
—not to generosity, but to self-denial,
not to patriotism, but to piety.

THOUGHTS

ON THE

MANNERS OF THE GREAT.

To a large and honourable class of the
community, to persons considerable in reputation, important by their condition in
life, and commendable for the decency of
their general conduct, these slight hints
are respectfully addressed. They are not
intended as a satire upon vice, or a ridicule
upon folly, being written neither for the
foolish nor the vicious. The subject is too
serious for ridicule; and those to whom it
is addressed are too respectable for satire.
It is recommended to the consideration of
those who, filling the higher ranks in life,

B

are naturally regarded as patterns, by which the manners of the rest of the world are to be fashioned.

The mass of mankind, in most places, and especially in those ,conditions of life which exempt them from the temptation to shameful vices, is, perhaps, chiefly composed of what is commonly termed, by the courtesy of the world, *good kind of people;* for persons of very flagitious wickedness are almost as rare as those of very eminent piety. To the latter of these, admonition were impertinent; to the former it were superfluous. These remarks, therefore, are principally written with a view to those persons of rank and fortune who live within the restraints of moral obligation, and acknowledge the truth of the Christian religion; and who, if in certain instances they allow themselves in practices not compatible with a strict profession of Christianity, seem to do it rather from habit and want of reflection, than either from disbelief of its doctrines, or contempt of its precepts.

Inconsideration, Fashion, and the World, are three confederates against Virtue, with whom even good kind of people often contrive to live on excellent terms: and the fair reputation which may be obtained by a complaisant conformity to the prevailing practice, and by mere decorum of manners, without a strict attention to religious' principle, is a constant source of danger to the rich and great. There is something almost irresistibly seducing in the contagion of general example: hence the necessity of that vigilance, which it is the business of Christianity to quicken by incessant admonition, and which it is the business of the world to lay asleep by the perpetual opiates of ease and pleasure.

A fair reputation is among the laudable objects of human ambition; yet even this really valuable blessing is sometimes converted into a snare, by inducing a treacherous security as soon as it is obtained; and by leading him who is too anxious about obtaining it, to stop short without aiming

at a higher motive of action. A fatal indolence is apt to creep in upon the soul
when it has once acquired the good opinion
of mankind, if the acquisition of that good
opinion was the ultimate end of its endeavours. Pursuit is at an end when the object is in possession; for he is not likely to
" press forward" who thinks he has already
" attained." The love of worldly reputation, and the desire of God's favour,
have this specific difference, that in the latter, the possession always augments the
desire; and the spiritual mind accounts
nothing done while any thing remains un-
done.

But after all, a fair fame, the support
of numbers, and the flattering concurrence
of human opinion, is obviously a deceitful
dependance; for, as every individual must
die for himself, and answer for himself,
both these imaginary resources will fail,
just at the moment when they could have
been of any use. A good reputation,
even without internal piety, would be

worth obtaining, if the tribunal of heaven were fashioned after the manner of human courts of judicature. If, at the general judgment, we were to be tried by a jury of our fellow mortals, it would be but common prudence to secure their favour at any price. But it can stand us in little stead in the great day of decision; it being the consummation of infinite goodness not to abandon us to the mercy of each other's sentence; but to reserve us for *his* final judgment, who knows every motive of every action; who will make strict inquisition into singleness of heart, and uprightness of intention; in whose eyes the sincere prayer of powerless benevolence will outweigh the most splendid profession, or the most dazzling action.

We cannot but rejoice in every degree of human virtue which operates favourably on society, whatever be the motive, or whoever be the actor; and we should gladly commend every degree of goodness, though it be not exactly squared by our own rules and notions.. Even the good actions of such persons as are too much actuated by a regard to appearances, are not without their beneficial effects. The righteousness of those who occupy this middle region of morality among us, certainly exceeds the righteousness of the Scribes and Pharisees, for they are not only exact in ceremonials, but, in many respects, fulfil the weightier matters of law and conscience. Like Herod, they often " hear gladly," and " do many "things." Yet I am afraid I shall be thought severe in remarking, that, in general, those characters in the New Testament, of whose future condition no very comfortable hope is given, seem to have been taken, not from the profligate, the abandoned, and the dishonourable; but from that decent class, commonly described by the term of *good sort of people;* that mixed kind of character in which virtue appears, if it do not predominate. The young Ruler was certainly one of the first of this order; and yet we are left in dark uncertainty as to his

final allotment. The rich man who built
him barns and storehouses, and only proposed to himself the full enjoyment of that
fortune, which we do not hear was unfair-
ly acquired, might have been, for all that
appears to the contrary, a *very good sort of
man;* at least, if we may judge of him by
multitudes who live precisely for the same
purposes, and yet enjoy a good degree of
credit, and who are rather considered as
objects of respect, than of censure. His
plan, like theirs, was " to take his ease, to
" eat, drink, and be merry."

But the most alarming instance is that of
the splendid epicure, who was cloathed in
purple and fine linen, and fared sumptuously
every day. He committed no enormities
that have been transmitted to us; for that
he dined well and dressed well, could hardly
incur the bitter penalty of eternal misery.
That his expences were suitable to his
station, and his splendour proportioned to
his opulence, does not exhibit any objection to his character. Nor are we told

that he refused the crumbs which Lazarus solicited. And yet this man, on an authority which we are not permitted to question, is represented, in a future state, as *lifting up his eyes being in torments.* His punishment seems to have been the consequence of an irreligious, a worldly, spirit; a heart corrupted by the softnesses and delights of life. It was not because he was rich, but because he trusted in riches; or, if even he was charitable, his charity wanted that principle which alone could sanctify it. His views terminated here; this world's good, and this world's applause, were the motives and the end of his actions. He forgot God; he was destitute of piety; and the absence of this great and first principle of human actions rendered his shining deeds, however they might be admired among men, of no value in the sight of God.

There is no error more common, or more dangerous, than the notion that an unrestrained indulgence of pleasure,

and an unbounded gratification of the
appetites are generally attended with a
liberal, humane, and merciful temper.—
Nor is there any opinion more false and
more fatal, or which demands to be more
steadily controverted, than, that libertinism
and good-nature are natural and necessary
associates.   For, after all that corrupt
poets, and more corrupt philosophers, have
told us of the blandishments of pleasure,
and of its tendency to soften the temper,
and humanize the affections, it is certain,
that nothing hardens the heart like excessive and unbounded luxury; and he who
refuses the fewest gratifications to his own
voluptuousness, will generally be found
the least susceptible of tenderness for the
wants of others.   In one reign, the cru-
elties at Rome bore an exact proportion
to the dissoluteness at Capreæ.   And,
in another, it is not less notorious, that
the imperial fiddler became more barbarous, as he grew more profligate.   Prosperity, says the Arabian proverb, fills the

heart till it makes it hard; and the most dangerous pits and snares for human virtue, are those which are so covered over with the flowers of prosperous fortune, that it requires a cautious foot, and a vigilant eye, to escape them.

Ananias and Sapphira were, perhaps, well esteemed in society; for it was enough to establish a very considerable reputation to sell even part of their possessions for religious purposes : but what an alarm does it sound to hypocrisy, that, instead of being rewarded for what they brought, they were punished for what they kept back! And it is to be feared, that this deceitful pair are not the only one, upon whom a good action, without a pure intention, has drawn down a righteous retribution.

Outward actions are the surest, and, indeed, to human eyes, the only evidences of sincerity; but Christianity is a religion of *motives* and *principles.* The Gospel is continually referring to the *heart*, as the source of good; it is to the poor in *spirit*, to the pure in *heart*, that the divine bles- sing is annexed.

A man may correct many improper practices, and refrain from many immoral actions, from merely human motives; but, though this partial amendment is not without its uses, yet this is only attack- ing symptoms, and neglecting the mortal disease. But, to subdue a worldly temper, to control irregular desires, and to have " a clean heart," is to attack sin in its strong holds. Totally to *accomplish* this, is, perhaps, beyond the narrow limits of human perfection, the best men being con- stantly humbled to find, that when they " would do good evil is present with them;" but to *attempt* it, with an humble reliance on superior aid, is so far from being an extravagant or romantic flight of virtue, that it is but the common duty of every ordinary Christian. And this perfection is not the less real, because it is a point which seems constantly to recede from our approaches, just as the sensible horizon recedes from our natural eye. Our highest attainments, instead of bringing us, " to the mark," only teach us that the mark is at a greater distance, by giving us more humbling views of ourselves, and more exalted conceptions of the state, after which we are labouring. Though the progress towards perfection may be perpetual in this world, the actual attainment is reserved for a better. And this restless desire of a happiness which we cannot reach, and this lively idea of a perfection which we cannot attain, are among the many arguments for a future state, which seem to come little short of demonstration. The humble Christian takes refuge under the deep sense of his disappointments and defects, in this consoling hope, " When I awake up after thy " likeness I shall be satisfied."

Let me not here be misunderstood as undervaluing the virtues which even worldly men may possess. Who is not charmed with humanity, generosity, and integrity, in whomsoever they may be found? But one virtue must not intrench upon another. Charity must not supplant faith. If a man be generous, good-natured, and humane, it is impossible not to feel for him the tenderness of a brother; but if, at the same time, he be irreligious, intemperate, or profane, who shall dare to say he is in a safe state? Good humour, and generous sentiments, will always make a man a pleasant acquaintance; but who shall lower the doctrines of the Gospel, to accommodate them to the conduct of men? Who shall bend a strait rule, to favour a crooked practice? Who shall controvert that authority which has said, that *without holiness no man shall see the Lord?*

. May I venture to be a little paradoxical; and while so many grave persons are descanting on the mischiefs of vice, may I be permitted to say a word on the mischiefs of virtue, or, rather, of that shining counterfeit, which, while it wants the specific gravity, has much of the brightness of sterling worth? Never, perhaps, did any age produce more beautiful declamations in praise of virtue than the present; never were more polished periods, rounded in honour of humanity. An antient Pagan would imagine that Astrea had returned to take up her abode in our metropolis; a primitive Christian would conclude, that " righteousness and peace " had there met together." But how would they be surprised to find that the obligation to these duties was not always thought binding, not only on the reader but on the eloquent encomiasts themselves! How would they be surprised to find that universal benevolence may subsist with partial injustice, and boundless liberality with sordid selfishness! that a man may seem eager in redressing the injuries of half the globe, without descending to the petty detail of private virtues; and burn with zeal for the good

of millions he never saw, while he is
spreading vice and ruin through the little
circle of his own personal influence!

When the general texture of an irregular life is spangled over with some constitutional pleasing qualities; when gaiety,
good humour, and a thoughtless pro-
fusion of expence, throw a lustre round
the faultiest characters, it is no wonder
that common observers are blinded into
admiration; a profuse generosity dazzles
them more than the fulfilment of all the
duties of the decalogue. But though it
may be a very good electioneering virtue,
and may promote the interests of the
candidate more than the whole catalogue
of evangelical graces; yet there are many
qualities which may obtain popularity
among men, who it do not tend to secure
the favour of God. It is somewhat strange
that the extravagance of the great should
be the criterion of their goodness with
those very people who are themselves the
victims to this idol; for the prodigal

pays no debts if he can help it. And it is a notorious instance of the danger of these popular virtues, and of the false judgments of men, that, in one of the wittiest and most popular comedies * which this country has ever produced, those very passages which exalt liberality, and turn justice into ridicule, were nightly applauded with enthusiastic rapture by those deluded tradesmen, whom, perhaps, that very sentiment helped to keep out of their money.

There is another sort of fashionable character, whose false brightness is still more pernicious, by casting a splendour over the most destructive vices. Corrupt manners, ruinous extravagance, and the most fatal passion for play, are sometimes gilded over with many engaging acts of charity, and a general attention and respect to the ceremonials of Religion. But this is degrading the venerable image and super-

---

* The School for Scandal.

scription of Christianity, by stamping
them on a baser metal than they were
ever intended to impress. The young
and gay shelter themselves under such
examples, and scruple the less to adopt the
bad parts of such mixed characters, when
they see that a loose and negligent, not to
say immoral conduct, is so compatible with
a religious profession.

But I digress from my intention; for it
is not the purpose of this address to take
notice of any actions which the common
consent of mankind has determined to be
wrong : but of such chiefly as are practised
by the sober, the decent, and the regular ;
and to drop a few hints on such less obvious
offences as are, in general,

Safe from the bar, the pulpit, and the throne.

Nor will the bounds which I have prescribed myself allow of my wandering into a
wide and general field of observation.

The idea of the present slight performance was suggested by reading the King's

c

late excellent proclamation against irreligion and immorality.* Under the shelter of so high a sanction, it may not be unseasonable to press on the hearts of the better disposed, such observances as seem to be generally overlooked, and to remark such offences as commonly elude censure, because they are not commonly thought censurable.

It is obvious to all pious persons, that that branch of the divine law, against which the better kind of people trespass with the least scruple, is the fourth commandment. Many who would shudder at the violation of the other nine, seem without ceremony to expunge this from the divine code; but by what authority they do this, has never been explained. The Christian legislator does not seem to have abridged the commandments; and there is no subsequent

* This Tract was written soon after the institution of the society for enforcing the King's proclamation against vice and irreligion.

-authority so much as pretended to by Pro-
testants. -

. It is not here intended to take notice of
such flagrant offences as lie open to the
cognizance of higher tribunals; or to pol-
lute this paper with descanting on the
holders of card assemblies on Sundays ; the
frequenters of taverns and gaming houses ;
the printers of Sunday newspapers ; the
proprietors of Sunday stage coaches ;* and
others who openly insult the laws of the
lands ; laws which will always be held sacred
by good subjects, even were not the law of
God antecedent to them.

Many of the order whom I here address
are persons of the tenderest humanity, and
not only wish well to the interest of virtue,
but are favourably disposed to advance the
cause of religion ; nay, would be extremely

* It is with deep concern that the Author is driven to
remark the monstrous increase of these two evils since
this Tract was published. The Sunday Newspapers have
multiplied nearly in the proportion of one to twenty, and
the stage coach drivers have lost all distinction of the day.

startled at not being thought sincerely religious; yet from inconsideration, want of time, want of self-examination, want of a just sense of the high requirements of the Divine law, want of suspecting the deceitfulness of the human heart, sometimes allow themselves in inattentions and negligences which materially affect their own safety, and the comfort of others.

While an animated spirit of charity seems to be kindled among us; while there is a general disposition to instruct the ignorant, and to reform the vicious; we cannot help regretting that these amiable exertions should be counteracted, in some degree, by practices of a directly opposite tendency; trifling in their appearance, but serious in their effects.

There are still among us petty domestic evils, which seem too inconsiderable to claim redress. There is an aggrieved body of men in our very capital, whose spiritual hardships seem scarcely to have been taken.

into consideration,—I mean the HAIR
DRESSERS, on whom

The Sunday shines, no day of rest to them.

Is there not a peculiar degree of unkind-
ness in exercising such cruelty on the souls
of men, whose whole lives are employed in
embellishing our persons? And is it quite
conceivable how a lady's conscience is able
to make such nice distinctions, that she
would be shocked at the idea of sending
for her mantua-maker* or milliner, her car-
penter or mason, on a Sunday, while she
makes no scruple regularly to employ a
hair dresser?

Is it not almost ridiculous to observe the
zeal we have for doing good at a distance,
while we neglect the little, obvious, every-
day, domestic duties, which should seem to
solicit our immediate attention? But an action ever so right and praise-worthy which

* It is feared that since these pages were written the
scruple of sending for either is much diminishing.

is only to be periodically performed, at distant intervals, is less burthensome to corrupt nature, than an undeviating attention to such small, constant, right habits as are hostile to our natural indolence, and would be perpetually vexing and disturbing our self-love. The weak heart indulges its infirmity, by allowing itself intermediate omissions, and habitual neglects of duty; reposing itself for safety, on regular but remote returns of stated performances. It is less troubled to subscribe to the propagation of the Gospel in foreign parts, than to have daily prayers in our own families; and I am persuaded that there are multitudes of well-meaning people who would gladly contribute to a mission of Christianity to Japan or Otaheite, to whom it never occurred that the hair-dresser, whom they are every Sunday detaining from church, has a soul to be saved; that the law of the land co-operates with the law of God, to forbid their employing him; and that they have no right, either legal or moral, to this por-

tion of his time. The poor man himself,
perhaps, dares not remonstrate, for fear he
should be deprived of his employment for
the rest of the week. If there were no
other objection to a pleasurable Sunday
among the great and affluent, methinks
this single one might operate : would not a
devout heart be unwilling to rob a fellow-
creature of his time for devotion, or a
humane one of his hour of rest ? "Love
" worketh no ill to his neighbour, therefore
" love is the fulfilling of the Law."

It is strange that there should be so little
consistency in human conduct, that the
same persons should gladly contribute to
spread the life of Christianity in another
hemisphere; while, by their example, they
actually obstruct the progress of it at home.
But it is, I doubt not, much oftner owing
to the imperceptible influence of custom
and habit, than to a decided ill attention.
Besides, it may be in morals as it is in
optics, the eye and the object may come
too close to each other, to answer the end

of vision. There are certain faults which press too near our self-love to be even perceptible to us.

The petty mischief of what is called *card money*, is so assimilated to our habits, and interwoven with our family arrangements, that even many of the prudent and the virtuous no longer consider it as a worm which is feeding on the vitals of domestic virtue. How many poor youths, after having been trained in a wholesome dread of idleness and gaming, when they are sent abroad into the world, are astonished to find that part of the wages of the servant is to be paid by his furnishing the implements of diversion for the guests of the master. Thus good servants are a commodity which has long been diminishing by an elaborate system. The more sober the family, the fewer attractions it must necessarily have; for these servants will naturally quit a place, however excellent, where there is no play, for one where there is some; and a family where there is but little, for one where there is much. Thus if the advantage of the dependant is to increase in a direct ratio to the dissipation of his employer, what encouragement is left for valuable servants, or what prospect remains of securing valuable servants for sober-minded families?

It will be said, that so small an evil is scarcely worth insisting on. But a small fault, which is become a part of a system, in time establishes an error into a principle. And that remonstrance which should induce people to abolish one wrong habit, or pluck out one rooted error, however trifling, would be of more real use than the most eloquent declamation against vice in general. To take out only one thorn from a suffering patient is more beneficial to him than the most elaborate disquisition on the pain he is suffering from the thorns which remain.

It should be held as an eternal truth, that what is morally wrong can never be politically right. It would be arguing great ignorance of human nature, and exacting a very rigorous degree of virtue from a per-

son of vulgar sentiments to expect that he
should wish well to the interests of sobriety,
or heartily desire the decrease of dissipation,
while the growth of it is made so profitable
to himself. It is requiring too much to
make the temptation so forcible where the
power of resistance is so weak. To hold
out to a poor fellow the strong seduction of
interest, and yet to expect he will retain
the same inflexible principle, is to expect,
from an illiterate servant, an elevation of
virtue, which has not always been found
even in statesmen and ministers.

It is not here intended to enter into any
animadversion on the subject of play itself.
But may we not ask, without offence, if it
be perfectly right to introduce any money
arising from, or connected with it, into a
part of regular family economy? Is it
not giving an air of system to diversion,
which does not seem entirely of a piece
with the other orderly practices of many
discreet families, where this odd traffic is
carried on? Would not our ancestors, -

who seem to have understood œconomy,
and magnificence too, at least as well as
their descendants, have been scandalized
had it been proposed to them to incorporate
play so intimately with the texture of their
domestic arrangements, as that it should
make part of their plan? And would they
have thought it a very dignified practice
not to have paid themselves for the amusements of their own houses; but to have in-
vited their friends to an entertainment of
which the guests were to defray part of
the expence?

Let me suppose a case: what appearance
would it have, if every gentleman who has
partaken of the social entertainment of a
friend's table, were, after dinner, expected, by the butler, to leave a piece of
money under his plate to pay for his wine?
Do not common sense, hospitality, friendship, and liberal feelings, revolt at the bare
suggestion of such a project? Yet there is,
in effect, as little hospitality, as little friendship, and as little liberality, in being obliged

to pay for the cards as for the wine; both equally making a part of the entertainment.

It is hardly too ludicrous to add, that, seeing how this point has been carried in favour of the groom of the chambers, (and it descends down to the lowest footman) we need not despair of seeing the butler insist on being allowed to furnish the wine, for which he shall compel the guests to pay, with the same high interest with which they now pay for the cards. It will seem odd at first, but afterwards we shall think no more about it, to see him, during dinner, noting down those who drink the more costly wines, that they may be taxed double. And it will sound whimsical *at first*, to hear the butler give his master notice, that he must quit his place, because the company have drank little wine. This only sounds ridiculous, while the leaving a place through deficiency of card money sounds reasonable, because we are accustomed to the one, and the other is not yet become fashionable.

The extinction of this favorite perquisite would at first be considered as a violent innovation. All reformations seem formidable before they are attempted. The custom of *vails*, " which gave corruption " *broader* wings to fly," was supposed to be invincible. Yet how soon did a general concurrence exterminate it! Had any one foretold, twenty years ago, that in a very short space near half a million of pilfering, swearing, sabbath-breaking children, should be rescued from the streets, and brought into habits of sobriety and virtue, should we not have laughed to scorn the spiritual Hercules, who would have undertaken that the cleansing stream of religious instruction should thus be poured through the Augean stable of ignorance and vice, and in some measure wash away its grossest impurities?

The servant would probably complain of the annihilation of this gainful custom: but the master would find his account in

indemnifying the loss; for he in his turn
would be released from the preposterous
contribution to the wages of other men's
servants. If in a family of overgrown dissipation the stated addition should not be
found equivalent to the relinquished perquisite, the servant must heroically submit
to the disadvantageous commutation for
the public good. And after all it would
be no very serious grievance if his reduced
income should not then exceed that of the
Chaplain. It will still at least exceed that
of many a deserving gentleman, bred to
liberal learning, whose feelings that learning
has refined to a painful acuteness, and who
is withering away in hopeless penury with
a large family, on a Curacy, but little sur-
passing the wages of a livery servant.

The same principle in human nature by
which the nabob, the contractor, and
others, by a sudden influx of unaccustomed
wealth, become voluptuous, extravagant,
and insolent, seldom fails to produce the
same effect on persons in these humbler

stations, when raised from inferior places to the sudden affluence of these gainful ones. Increased profligacy on a sudden swell of fortune is commonly followed by desperate methods to improve the circum-stances when impaired by the improvidence attending unaccustomed prosperity.

There is another domestic practice which it is almost idle to mention, because it is so difficult to redress, since such is the present state of society that even the conscientious think themselves obliged to concur in it. That ingenuity which could devise some effectual substitute for the daily and hourly lie of *Not at home*, would deserve well of society. Why will not some of those illustrious ladies who lead in the fashionable world invent some phrase which shall equally rescue from destruction the time of the master and the veracity of the servant? Some new and appropriate expression, the not adopting which should be branded with the stigma of vulgarity, might accomplish that which the charge of its being immoral has failed to accomplish.

The expediency of the denial itself, no
one will dispute, who has a just idea of the
value of time.   Some scrupulous persons so
very much dispute the lawfulness of making
their servants' tongue the medium of any
kind of falsehood, as to make it a point of
conscience rather to lay themselves open to
the irruption of every idle invader, who
sallies out on morning visits bent on the
destruction of business and the annihilation
of study.   People of very strict integrity
lament that this practice induces a general
spirit of lying, mixes itself with the habit,
and by a quality, the reverse of an alterative,
gradually undermines the moral constitution.—Others on the contrary assert, that
this is one of those lies of convention, no
more intended to deceive, than the *dear sir*
at the beginning, or your *humble servant* at
the close of a letter to a person who is not
dear to you, and to whom you owe no sub-
jection.   There is, however, this very material difference, that if the first be a falsehood, you do not convey it by proxy : You

use it yourself, and you use it to one who sets no more value on your words than you intended he should; and who shews you he does not, by using the same stated phrase in return, in addressing you, for whom he cares as little. Here the words pass for no more than they are worth.

The ill effects of the custom we are lamenting may be traced in marking the gradual initiation of an unpractised country servant. And who has not felt for his virtuous distress, when he has been ordered to call back a more favoured visitant, whom he had just sent away with the assurance that his lady was not at home? Who has not seen his suppressed indignation at being obliged to become himself the detector of that falsehood of which he had been before the instrument? But a little practice and a repetition of reproof for even daring to *look* honest, soon cures this fault, especially as he is sure to be commended, in proportion to the increased firmness of his voice, and the steadiness of his countenance.

D

If this evil, petty as it may seem to be, be really without a remedy; if the state of society be such that it cannot be redressed, let us not be so unreasonable as to expect that a servant will equivocate in small instances and not in great ones. To hope that he will always lie for your convenience, and never for his own, is perhaps expecting more from human nature, in a low and uncultivated state, than we have any right to expect. Nor should the master look for undeviating and perfect rectitude from his servant, in whom the principle of veracity is daily and hourly weakened in conformity to his own command.

Let us bring home the case to ourselves, the only fair way of determining in all cases of conscience. Suppose that we had established it into a system to allow ourselves regularly to lie on one certain, given subject, every day, and every hour in the day; while we continued to value ourselves on the most undeviating adherence to truth on every other point. Who shall say, that at

the end of one year's tolerated and syste
matic lying, on this individual subject, we
should continue to look upon falsehood in
general with the same abhorrence we did
when we first entered upon this partial exercise of it.

There is an evil newly crept into polished
society, and it comes under a mask so specious, that they who are allured by it,
come not seldom under the description of
Good sort of people. I allude to SUNDAY
CONCERTS. Many who would be startled
at a profane, or even a light amusement,
allow themselves to fancy that the name of
sacred music sanctifies the diversion. But
if those more favoured beings, whom Providence enables to live in ease and affluence,
do not make these petty renunciations of
their own ways, and their own pleasure,
what criterion have we by which to judge
of their sincerity? For as the goodness of
Providence has exempted them from painful occupations, they have neither labour
from which to rest, nor business from which

to refrain. A little abstinence from pleasure is the only valid evidence they have
to give of their obedience to the divine
precept.

I know with what indignant scorn this
remark will, by many, be received: I
know that much will be advanced in favour
of the sanctity of this amusement. I shall
be told that the words are, many of them,
extracted from the Bible, and that the composition is the divine Handel's. But were
the angel Gabriel the poet, the archangel
Michael the composer, and the song of the
Lamb the subject, it would not abrogate
that statute of the Most High, which has
said, " Thou shalt keep holy the Sabbath
" day, and thy SERVANT, and thy CATTLE,
" shall do no manner of work."—I am persuaded that the hallelujahs of heaven would
make no moral music to the ear of a conscientious person, while he reflected that
multitudes of servants are through this
means waiting in the street, exposed to every
temptation; engaged, perhaps, in profane

swearing, and idle, if not dissolute conversation: and the very cattle are deprived of
that rest which the tender mercy of God
was graciously pleased, by an astonishing
condescension, to include in the commandment.

But I will, for the sake of argument, so
far concede as to allow of the innocence
and even piety of Sunday concerts: I will
suppose (what, however, does not often
happen) that no unhallowed strains are
ever introduced; I will admit that some attend these concerts with a view to cultivate
devout affections; that they cherish the serious impressions excited by the music, and
retire in such a frame of spirit as convinces
them that the heart was touched while the
ear was gratified: nay, I *would* grant, if
such a concession would be accepted, that
the intervals were filled up with conversation, " whereby one may edify another :"—
yet all these good effects, allowing them
really to have been produced, will not remove the invincible objection of an EVIL EX-

AMPLE; and what liberal spirit would refuse any reasonable sacrifice of its own pleasure to so important a motive? Your servants have been accustomed to consider a
concert as a secular diversion; if you,
therefore, continue it on a Sunday, will
not they also expect to be indulged on that
day with their common amusements? Saint
Paul, who was a very liberal thinker, believed it prudent to make frequent sacrifices
of things indifferent in themselves. He
was willing to deny himself a harmless and
lawful gratification, *even as long as the world
stood*, rather than shock the tender consciences of men of less understanding.
Where a practice is neither good nor evil in
itself, it is both discreet and generous to
avoid it, if it can be attended with any
possible danger to minds less enlightened,
and to faith less confirmed.

But religion apart, I have sometimes
wondered that people do not yield to the
temptation that is held out to them, of abstaining from diversions one day in seven,

upon motives of mere human policy; as
voluptuaries sometimes fast, to give a
keener relish to the delights of the next
repast: for pleasure, like an over-fed lamp,
is extinguished by the excess of its own
aliment: not to say that the instrument of
our gratification is often converted into our
bane. Anacreon was choaked by a grape
stone. The lovers of pleasure are not
always prudent, even upon their own principles; for I am persuaded that this world
would afford much more real satisfaction
than it does, if we did not press, and tor-
ture, and strain it, in order to make it yield
what it does not contain : Much good, and
much pleasure, it does liberally bestow ;
but no labour, or art, can extract from it
that elixir of peace, that divine essence of
content, which it is not in its nature to produce. There is good sense in searching into
every blessing for its *hidden* properties;
but it is folly to ransack and plunder it for
such properties as the experience of all ages
tell us are *foreign* to it. We exhaust the

world of its pleasures, and then lament that it is empty ; we wring those pleasures to the very dregs, and then complain that they are vapid. We erroneously seek in the world for that peace which we are repeatedly told is not to be found in it. While we neglect to seek it in *Him* who has expressly told us that *our* happiness depends on *his* having " overcome the world."— " Peace I leave with you, my peace I give " unto you ; not as *the world giveth give I* " *unto you.*"

I shall, probably, be accused of a very narrow and fanatical spirit, in animadverting on a practice so little suspected of harm as the frequenting of public walks and gardens on a Sunday, and, certainly there cannot be an amusement more entirely harmless in itself. But I must appeal to the honest testimony of our own hearts, if the *effect* be favourable to seriousness. Do we commonly retire from these places with the impression which were made on us at church in their full force? We entered these sprightly scenes, perhaps, with a strong

remaining tincture of that devout spirit
which the public worship had infused into
the mind : but have we not felt it gradually
diminish? Have not our powers of resistance grown insensibly weaker? Has not the
gaity of the scenes converted, as it were,
argument into illusion? The doctrines,
which in the morning appeared the sober
dictates of reason, now seem unreasonably
rigid; and truths, which were then thought
incontrovertible, now appear impertinent.
To answer objections is much easier than to
withstand allurements. The understanding
may controvert a startling proposition with
less difficulty than the sliding heart can resist the infection of seducing gaity. To
oppose a cold and speculative faith to the
enchantment of present pleasure, is to fight
with inadequate weapons; it is resisting
arms with rules; it is combating a temptation with an idea. Whereas, he who en-
gages in the Christian warfare, will find
that his chief strength consists in knowing
that he is very weak; his progress will de-

pend on his conviction that he is every
hour liable to go back; his success, on the
persuasion of his fallibility; his safety, on
the assurance that to retreat from danger is
his highest glory, and to decline the combat
his truest courage.

Whatever indisposes the mind for the
duty of any particular season, though it
assume ever so innocent a form, cannot be
perfectly right. If the heart be laid open
to the incursion of vain imaginations, and
worldly thoughts, it matters little by what
gate the enemy entered. If the effect be
injurious, the cause cannot be quite harmless. It is the perfidious property of certain
pleasures, that, though they seem not to
have the smallest harm in themselves, they
imperceptibly indispose the mind to every
thing that is good.

Many readers will be apt to produce
against all this preciseness, that hackneyed
remark which one is tired of hearing, that
Sunday diversions are allowed publicly in
many foreign countries, as well in those

professing the reformed religion, as popery.
But the corruptions of one part of the Protestant world are no reasonable justification
of the evil practices of another. Error and
infirmity can never be proper objects of
imitation. It is still a remnant of the old
leaven: and as to pleading the practice of
Roman Catholic countries, one blushes to
hear an enlightened Protestant justifying
himself by examples drawn from that be-
nighted religion, whose sanctions we should
in any other instance be ashamed to plead.

Besides, though I am far from vindicating
the amusements permitted on Sundays in
foreign countries, by allowing that established custom and long prescription have
the privilege of conferring right; yet fo-
reigners may, at least, plead the sanction of
custom, and the connivance of the law:
while in this country, the law of the land
and established usage, concurring with still
higher motives, give a sort of venerable
sanction to religious observances, the breach
of which will be always more liable to mis-

construction than in countries where so
many motives do not concur in its support.

I do not assert that all those who neglect
a strict observation of the Lord's day are
remiss in the performance of all their other
duties: though they should bear in mind
that the observance of their other duties is
no atonement for the neglect of this; I
will however venture to affirm, that all
whom I have remarked conscientiously to
observe this day from right motives, have
been uniformly attentive to their general
conduct. It has been the opinion of many
wise and good men,* that Christianity will

* The testimony of one lawyer will, perhaps, be
less suspected than that of many priests. " I have
" ever found," says the great Lord Chief Justice Hale,
" by a strict and diligent observation, that a due ob-
" servance of the duty of Sunday has ever had joined
" to it a blessing upon the rest of my time; and the
" week that has been so begun has been blessed and
" prosperous to me: and, on the other side, when I
" have been negligent of the duties of this day, the
" rest of the week has been unsuccessful and unhappy
" to my own secular employments. So that I could

stand, or fall, as this day it neglected, or
observed. Sunday secms to be a kind of
Christian palladium; and the city of God
will never be totally taken by the enemy
till the observance of that be quite lost.
Every sincere soldier of the great Captain
of our Salvation must, therefore, exert
himself in its defence, as ever he would
preserve the divine Fort of Revelation
against the confederated attacks of the
world and the Devil.

I shall proceed to enumerate a few of the
many causes which seem to impede well-disposed people in the progress of religion.
None perhaps contributes more to it than
that cold, prudential caution against the
folly of aiming at *perfection*, so frequent in
the mouths of the wordly wise. " We
" must take the world," say they, " as we
" find it; reformation is not our business,

" easily make an estimate of my successes the week
" following, by the manner of my passing this day.
" AND I DO NOT WRITE THIS LIGHTLY, BUT BY
" LONG AND SOUND EXPERIENCE."

Sir Matthew Hale's Works.

" and we are commanded not to be righte-
" ous overmuch." A text by the way in-
tirely misunderstood and perverted by people of this sort. But these admonitions are
contrary to every maxim in human affairs.
In arts and letters* the most consummate
models are held out to imitation. We never
hear any body cautioned against becoming
too wise, too learned, or too rich. Activity
in business is accounted commendable; in
friendship it is amiable; in ambition it is
laudable. The highest exertions of industry
are commended; the finest energies of genius are admired. In all the perishing concerns of earthly things, zeal is extolled as
exhibiting marks of a sprightly temper and
a vigorous mind. Strange! that to be
" fervent in spirit," should only be disho-

---

* When Pliny the younger was accused of despising
the degenerate eloquence of his own age, and of the
vanity of aspiring at perfection in oratory, and of endeavouring to become the rival of Cicero; instead of
denying the charge, he exclaimed with a noble spirit,
" I think it the height of folly not always to propose
" to myself the most perfect object of imitation."

nourable in that single instance which
should seem to demand unremitting diligence and extinguishable warmth.

But after all, is an excessive and intemperate zeal the *common* vice of the times? Is
there any *very* imminent danger that the
enthusiasm of the great should transport
them to dangerous and inconvenient excesses? Are our young men of fashion so
very much led away by the fervours of
piety, that they require to have their imaginations tamed, and their ardours cooled
by the freezing maxims of worldly wisdom?
Is the spirit of the age so *very* much inclin-
ed to catch and communicate the fire of devotion, as to require to be damped by admonition, or extinguished by ridicule?
When the inimitable Cervantes attacked
the wild notions and romantic ideas which
misled the age in which he lived, he did
wisely, because he combated an actually
existing evil; but in this latter end of the
eighteenth century, there seems to be little
more occasion (among persons of rank, I

mean) of cautions against enthusiasm than
against chivalry; and he who declaims
against religious excesses in the company of
well-bred people, shews himself to be as
little acquainted with the manners of the
times in which he lives, as he would do who
should think it a point of duty to write
another Don Quixote.

Among the devices dangerous to our
moral safety, certain favourite and specious
maxims are not the least successful, as they
carry with them an imposing air of indulgent candour, and always seem to be on the
popular side of good-nature. One of the
most obvious of these is, that method of re-
conciling the conscience to practices not decidedly wicked, and yet not scrupulously
right, by the qualifying phrase, *that there is
no harm in it*. I am mistaken if more innocent persons do not inflame their spiritual
reckoning by this treacherous apology than
by almost any other means. Few are sys-
tematically, or premeditatedly wicked; or
propose to themselves, at first, more than

such small indulgences as they are persuaded *have no harm in them.* But this latitude is gradually and imperceptibly enlarged. As the expression is vague and indeterminate ; as the darkest shade of virtue, and the lightest shade of vice, melt into no very incongruous colouring ; as the bounds between good and evil are not always so precisely defined but that he who ventures to the confines of the one, will find himself on the borders of the other ; every one furnishes his own definition ; every one extends the supposed limits a little farther ; till the bounds which fence in permitted from unlawful pleasures are gradually broken down, and the marks which separated them imperceptibly destroyed.

It is, perhaps, one of the most alarming symptoms of the degeneracy of morals in the present day, that the distinctions of right and wrong are almost swept away in polite conversation. The most grave offences are often named with cool indifference ; the most shameful profligacy with affected ten-

E

derness and indulgent toleration. The sub-
stitution of the word *gallantry* for that crime
which stabs domestic happiness and conjugal
virtue, is one of the most dangerous of all
the modern abuses of language. Atrocious
deeds should never be called by gentle
names. This must certainly contribute,
more than any thing, to diminish the horror
of vice in the rising generation. That our
passions should be too often engaged on the
side of error, we may look for the cause,
though not for the vindication, in the unresisted propensities of our constitution; but
that our *reason* should ever be exerted in its
favor, that our *conversation* should ever be
taught to palliate it, that our *judgment*
should ever look on it with indifference,
that our tongues should ever be employed to
confound the eternal distinctions of right
and wrong; this has no shadow of excuse;
because this can pretend to no foundation
in nature, no apology in temptation, no
palliative in passion.

However defective, therefore, our practice

may be ; however we may be eluded by seduction, or precipitated by passion, let us beware of lowering the STANDARD of RIGHT. This induces an imperceptible corruption into the heart, stagnates the noblest principle of action, irrecoverably debases the sense of moral and religious obligation, and prevents us from living up to the height of our nature, because it prevents us from knowing its possible elevation. It cuts off all communication with virtue, and almost prevents the possibility of a return to it. If we do not rise as high as we aim, we shall rise the higher for having aimed at a lofty mark : but where the RULE is low, the practice cannot be high, though the converse of the proposition is not proportionably true.

Nothing more benumbs the exertions of ardent youthful virtue than the cruel sneer which worldly prudence bestows on active goodness, and the cool derision it expresses at the defeat of a benevolent scheme, of which malice, rather than penetration, had

foreseen the failure. Alas! there is little
need of any such discouragements. The
world is a climate which too naturally chills
a glowing generosity, and contracts an ex-
panded heart. The zeal of the most sanguine is but too apt to cool, and the activity
of the most diligent, to slacken of itself:
and the disappointments which Benevolence
encounters in the failure of her best-con-
certed projects, and the frequent depravity
of the most chosen objects of her bounty,
would soon dry up the amplest streams of
charity, where they not fed by the living
fountain of religious principle.

I cannot dismiss this part of my subject
without animadverting on the too prompt
alacrity, even of worthy people, to dissemi-
nate, in public and general conversation,
instances of their unsuccessful attempts to do
good. I never hear a charity story begun
to be related in mixed company, that I do not
tremble for the catastrophe, lest it should
exhibit some mortifying disappointment,
which may deter the inexperienced from

running any generous hazards, and excite
harsh suspicions, at an age, when it is less
dishonourable to meet with a few casual
hurts, and transient injuries, than to go
cased in the cumbersome and impenetrable
armour of distrust. The liberal should be
particularly cautious how they furnish the
avaricious with creditable pretences for sav‑
ing their money, since all the instances of the
mortifications the humane meet with are
carefully treasured up, and added to the
armory of the covetous man's arguments,
and never fail to be produced by him as de‑
fensive weapons, upon every fresh attack
on his heart or his purse.

But I am willing to hope that that un‑
charitableness which we so often meet with
in persons of advanced years, is not always
the effect of a heart naturally hard. Mi‑
santhropy is very often nothing but abused
sensibility. Long habits of the world, and
a melancholy conviction how little good he
has been able to do in it, harden many a
tender-hearted person. The milk of human

kindness becomes soured by repeated acts
of ingratitude. This commonly induces an
indifference to the well-being of others,
from a hopelessness of adding to the stock
of human virtue and human happiness.
This uncomfortable disease is very fond of
spreading its own contagion, which is a
cruelty to the health of young and unin-
fected virtue.—For this distemper, generat-
ed by a too sanguine disposition, and grown
chronical from repeated disappointments,
from having rated worldly virtue and
worldly generosity too highly, there is but
one remedy, or rather one prevention : and
this is a genuine principle of piety. He
who is once convinced that he is to assist
his fellow-creatures, because it is the will of
God ; he who is persuaded that his for-
giving his fellow-servant the hundred pence
is a condition annexed to the remission of
his own ten thousand talents, will soon get
above all uneasiness when the consequence
does not answer his expectation. He will
soon become only anxious to do his duty,

humbly committing events to higher hands.
Disappointments will then only serve to
refine his motives, and purify his virtue. His
charity will then become a sacrifice with
which God is well pleased ! His affections
will be more spiritualized, and his devotions
more intense. Nothing short of such a
courageous piety, growing on the stock of
Christian principle, can preserve a heart
hackneyed in the world from relaxed
diligence, or criminal d spair.

People in general are not aware of the
mischief of judging of the rightness of any
action by its prosperity, or of the excellence
of any institution by the abuse of it. We
must never proportion our exertions to our
success, but to our duty. If every laudable
undertaking were to be dropped because it
failed in some cases, or was abused in others,
there would not be left an Alms House, a
Charity-School, or an Hospital in the land.
If every right practice were to be discontinued because it had been found not to
be successful in every instance, and if every

right principle were rejected because it had not been operative in all cases, this false reasoning pushed to the extreme, might at last be brought as an argument for shutting up our churches, and burning our bibles.

But if, on the one hand, there is a proud and arrogant discretion which ridicules, as Utopian and romantic, every generous project of the active and the liberal; so there is on the other, a sort of popular bounty which arrogates to itself the exclusive name of *feeling*, and rejects with disdain the influence of an higher principle. I am far from intending to depreciate this humane and exquisitely tender sentiment which the beneficent Author of our nature gave us as a stimulus to remove the distresses of others, in order to get rid of our own uneasiness. I would only observe, that where not strengthened by superior motives, it is a casual and precarious instrument of good, and ceases to operate, except in the immediate presence, and within the audible cry

of misery. This sort of feeling forgets that
any calamity exists which is out of its own
sight; and though it would empty its purse
for such an occasional object as rouses transient sensibility, yet it seldom makes any
stated provision for miseries, which are not
the less real because they do not obtrude
upon the sight, and awaken the tenderness
of immediate sympathy. This is a mechanical charity, which requires springs and
wheels to set it a going; whereas real christian charity does not wait to be acted
upon by impressions and impulses.

Another cause which very much intimi-
dates well-disposed people, is their terror,
lest the character of piety should derogate
from their reputation as men of sense.
Every man of the world naturally arrogates
to himself the superiority of understanding
over every religious man. He, therefore,
who has been accustomed to set a high
value on his intellectual powers, must have
made very considerable advances in piety
before he can acquire a magnanimous indifference to this usurped superiority of ano-

ther : before he can submit to the parsimo-
nious allotment of wit and learning, which
is assigned him by the supercilious hand of
worldly wisdom. But this attack upon his
pride will be no bad touchstone of his sincerity. If his advances have not been so
considerable, then, by an hypocrisy of the
least common kind, he will be industrious
to appear less good than he really is, lest
the distinction of his serious propensities
should draw on him the imputation of ordinary parts or low attainments. But the
danger is, that while he is too sedulously
intent on maintaining his pretensions as an
ingenious man, his claims to piety should
daily become weaker. That which is long
suppressed is too frequently extinguished.

Nothing, perhaps, more plainly discovers
the faint impression which religion has really
made upon our hearts, than this disincli-
nation, even of good people, to serious conversation. Let me not be misunderstood;
I do not mean the wrangle of debate; I do
not mean the gall of controversy; I do not
mean the fiery strife of *opinions*, than which

nothing can be less favourable to good
nature, good manners, or good society. But
it were to be wished, that it was not thought
ill-bred and indiscreet, that the escapes of the
tongue should now and then betray the
" abundance of the heart:" that, when such
subjects are casually introduced, a discou-
raging coldness did not instantly take place
of that sprightly animation of countenance
which made common topics interesting. If
these " outward and visible signs" were
unequivocal, we should form but moderate
ideas of the " inward and spiritual grace."
It were to be wished, that such subjects
were not thought dull, *merely* because they
are good ; it were to be wished that they
had the common chance of fair discussion ;
and that parts and learning were not
ashamed to exert themselves on occasions
where both might appear to so much advantage. If the heart were really interested,
could the affections forbare now and then
to break out into language? Artists, phy-
sicians, merchants, lawyers, and scholars,

keep up the spirit of their professions by
mutual intercourse. New lights are struck
out, improvements are suggested, emulation
is kindled, love of the object is inflamed,
mistakes of the judgment are rectified, and
desire of excellence is excited by communication. And is piety alone so very easy of
acquisition, so very natural to our corrupt
hearts, as to require none of the helps
which are indispensable on all other subjects? Travellers, who are to visit any
particular country, are full of earnest
inquiry, and diligent research; they think
nothing indifferent by which their future
pleasure or advantage may be affected.
Every hint which may procure them any
information, or caution them against any
danger, is thankfully received; and all this,
because they are really in *earnest* in their
preparation for this journey; and do fully
believe, not only that there is such a country,
but that they themselves have a personal,
individual interest in the good, or evil,
which may be found in it.

A farther danger to *good kind of people* seems to arise from a mistaken idea, that only great and actual sins are to be guarded against. Whereas, in effect, temptations to the grosser sins do not so frequently occur to those who are hedged in by the blessings of affluence, by a regard to reputation and the care of health; while sins of omission make up, perhaps, the most formidable part of *their* catalogue of offences. These generally supply in number what they want in weight, and are the more dangerous for being little ostensible. They continue to be repeated with less regret, because the remembrance of their predecessors does not, like the remembrance of formal, actual crimes, assume a body and a shape, and terrify by the impression of particular scenes and circumstances. While the memory of transacted evil haunts a tender conscience by perpetual apparition; omitted duty, having no local or personal existence, not being recorded by standing acts and deeds, and dates, and having no distinct image to which the mind may recur, sinks into quiet oblivion, without deeply wounding the conscience, or tormenting the imagination. These omissions were, perhaps, among the "secret sins," from which the royal penitent so earnestly desired to be cleansed : and it is worthy of the most serious consideration, that these are the offences against which the Gospel pronounces some of its very alarming denunciations. It is not less against negative than against actual evil, that affectionate exhortation, lively remonstrance, and pointed parable, are exhausted. It is against the tree which bore no fruit, the lamp which had no oil, the unprofitable servant who made no use of his talent, that the severe sentence is denounced ; as well as against *corrupt* fruit, *bad* oil, and talents *ill* employed. We are led to believe, from the same high authority, that omitted duties and neglected opportunities, will furnish no inconsiderable portion of our future condemnation. A very awful part of the decision, in the great day of account, seems

to be reserved merely for carelessness,
omissions, and negatives. Ye gave me NO
meat ; ye gave me NO drink ; ye took me
NOT in ; ye visited me NOT. On the punishment attending positive crimes, as
being more naturally obvious, it was not,
perhaps, thought so necessary to insist.

Another cause, which still further im-
pedes the reception of Religion even among
the well-disposed, is, that garment of sad-
ness in which people delight to suppose her
dressed ; and that life of hard austerity, and
pining abstinence, which they pretend she
enjoins her disciples. And it were well if
this were only the misrepresentation of her
declared enemies ; but unhappily, it is the
too frequent misconception of her injudicious
friends. But such an over-charged picture
is not more unamiable than it is unlike : for
I will venture to affirm, that Religion,
with all her beautiful and becoming sanctity,
imposes fewer sacrifices, not only of rational,
but of pleasurable enjoyment, than the
uncontrolled dominion of any one vice.

Her service is not only safety hereafter, but freedom here. She is not so tyrannizing as appetite, so exacting as the World, nor so despotic as Fashion. Let us try the case by a parallel, and examine it, not as affecting our virtue, but our pleasure. Does Religion forbid the cheerful enjoyments of life as rigorously as Avarice forbids them? Does she require such sacrifices of our ease as Ambition, or such renunciations of our quiet as Pride? Does Devotion *murder sleep* like dissipation? Does she destroy Health like Intemperance? Does she annihilate Fortune like Gaming? Does she imbitter Life like Discord; or abridge it like Duelling? Does Religion impose more vigilance than Suspicion? or inflict half as many mortifications as Vanity? Vice has her martyrs: and the most austere and self-denying Ascetic (who mistakes the genius of Christianity almost as much as her enemies mistake it) never tormented himself with such cruel and causeless severity as that with which Envy lacerates her unhappy votaries. Worldly

honour obliges us to be at the trouble of
resenting injuries; and worldly prudence
obliges us to be at the expence of litigating
about them; but Religion spares us the in-
convenience of the one and the cost of the
other, by the summary command to forgive; and by this injunction she consults
our happiness no less than our virtue: for
the torment of constantly hating any one
must be, at least, equal to the sin of it.
And resentment is an evil so costly to our
peace that we should find it more cheap to
forgive even were it not more right. If
this estimate be fairly made, then is the
balance clearly on the side of Religion even
in the article of pleasure.

It is an infirmity not uncommon to *good
kind of people*, to comfort themselves that
they are living in the exercise of some one
natural good quality, and to make a religious merit of a constitutional happiness.
They have also a strong propensity to
separate what God has joined; belief and
practice; the creed and the command-

ments ; actions and motives ; moral duty
and religious obedience. Whereas, you
will hardly find, in all the New Testament,
a moral, or a social virtue that is not
hedged in by some religious injunction:
scarcely a good action enjoined towards
others, but it is connected with some
exhortation to personal purity.. All the
charities of benevolence are, in general, so
agreeable to the natural make of the heart,
that it is a very tender mercy of God to
have made that a duty, which, to finer
spirits, would have been irresistible as an inclination; and to have annexed the highest
future reward to the greatest present pleasure. But in order to give a religious
sanction to a social virtue, the duty of
" visiting the fatherless and widow in their
" affliction," is inseparably attached to
the difficult and self-denying injunction of
" keeping ourselves unspotted from the
" world." This adjunct is the more need-
ful, as many are apt to make a kind of
moral commutation, and to allow them-

selves so much pleasure in exchange for so
much charity. They think they may fairly
pay themselves for abstinence from one
fault by indulgence in another. But the
Christian virtues derive their highest lustre
from association : they have such a spirit of
society, that they are weak and imperfect
when solitary ; their radiance is brightened
by an intermingling of their beams, and
their natural strength multiplied by their
alliance with each other.

It cannot be denied that *good sort of people*
sometimes use religion as the voluptuous
use physic. As the latter employ medi-
cine to make health agree with luxury, the
former consider religion as a medium to
reconcile peace of conscience with a life of
pleasure. But no moral chemistry can
blend natural contradictions. In all such
unnatural mixtures the world will still be
uppermost, and religion will disdain to
coalesce with its antipathy.

Let me not be suspected of intending to
insinuate that religion encourages men to

fly from society, and hide themselves in
solitudes : to renounce the generous and
important duties of active life, for the
visionary, cold, and fruitless virtues of an
Hermitage, or a Cloyster. No : the mischief arises not from our living in the world,
but from the world living in us; occu-
pying our hearts, and monopolizing our
affections. Action is the life of virtue, and
the world is the theatre of action. Perhaps
some of the most perfect patterns of human
conduct may be found in the most public
stations, and among the busiest orders of
mankind. It is, indeed, a scene of trial,
but the glory of the triumph is proportioned
to the peril of the conflict. A sense of
danger quickens circumspection, and makes
virtue more vigilant. Lot, perhaps is not
the only character who maintained his integrity in a great city, proverbially wicked,
and forfeited it in the bosom of retirement.

It has been said that worldly *good sort of
people* are a greater credit to their profession,
by exhibiting more cheerfulness, gaiety,

and happiness, than are visible in serious
Christians. If this assertion be true, which
I very much suspect, is it not probable that
the apparent ease and gaiety of the former
may be derived from the same source of
consolation which Mrs. Quickly recom-
mends to Falstaff, in Shakespeare's admirable picture of the death-bed scene of
that witty profligate? " He wished for
" comfort, quoth mine hostess, and began
" to talk of God; now I to comfort him,
" begged him he should not think of God :
" it was time enough to trouble himself
" with these things." Do not many deceive themselves by drawing water from
these dry wells of comfort? and patch up
a precarious and imperfect happiness in
this world, by diverting their attention
from the concerns of the next?

Another obstruction to the growth of
piety, is that unhappy prejudice which
even good kind of people too often entertain against those who differ from them in
opinion. Every man who is sincerely in

earnest to advance the interests of religion, will have acquired such a degree of candour, as to become indifferent by whom good is done, or who has the reputation of doing it, provided it be actually done. He will be anxious to increase the stock of human virtue, and of human happiness, by every possible means. He will whet and sharpen every instrument of goodness, though it be not cast in his own mould, or fashioned after his own pattern. He will never consider whether the form suits his own particular taste, but whether the instrument itself be calculated to accomplish the work of his master.

I shall conclude these loose and immethodical hints with a plain, tho' short address to those who content themselves with a decent profession of the doctrines, and a formal attendance on the offices, instead of a diligent discharge of the duties of Christianity. Believe, and forgive me!—you are the people who lower religion in the eyes of its enemies. The openly profane, the avowed enemies to God and goodness, serve to confirm the truths they mean to oppose, to illustrate the doctrines they deny, and to accomplish the very predictions they affect to disbelieve. But you, like an inadequate and faithless prop, overturn the edifice which you pretend to support.—When an acute and keen-eyed infidel measures your lives with the rule by which you profess to walk; he finds so little analogy between them, the copy is so unlike the pattern, that this inconsistency of yours is the pass through which his most dangerous attack is made. And I must confess, that, of all the arguments, which the malignant industry of infidelity has been able to muster, the negligent conduct of professing Christians seems to me to be the only one which is really capable of staggering a man of sense.—He hears of a spiritual and self-denying religion; he reads the beatitudes; he observes that the grand artillery of the Gospel is planted against pride and sensuality. He then turns to the transcript of

this perfect original; to the lives which
pretend to be fashioned by it. There he
sees, with triumphant derision, that pride,
self-love, luxury, self-sufficiency, unbounded personal expence, and an inordinate
appetite for pleasure, are reputable vices in
the eyes of many of those who acknowledge
the truth of the Christian doctrines. He
weighs that meekness to which a blessing
is promised, with that arrogance which is
too common to be very dishonourable.
He compares' that non-conformity to the
world, which the Bible makes the criterion
of a believer, with that rage for amusement which is not considered as disreputable
in a Christian. He opposes the self-denying and lowly character of the Author of
our faith with the sensual practices of his
followers. He finds little resemblance between the restraints prescribed, and the
gratifications indulged in. What conclusions must a speculative, reasoning sceptic
draw from such premises? Is it any wonder
that such phrases as " a broken spirit," a

" contrite heart," " poverty of spirit,"
" refraining the soul," " keeping it low,"
and " casting down high imaginations,"
should be to the unbeliever " foolishness,"
when such humiliating doctrines are a
" stumbling block" to professing Christians; to Christians who cannot cordially
relish a religion which professedly tells them
it was sent to stain the pride of human
glory, and " to exclude boasting?"

But though the passive and self-denying
virtues are not high in the esteem of mere
good sort of people, yet they are peculiarly
the evangelical virtues. The world extols
brilliant actions; the Gospel enjoins good
habits and right motives: it seldom inculcates those splendid deeds which make
heroes, or teaches those lofty sentiments
which constitute philosophers; but it enjoins
the harder task of renouncing self, of living
uncorrupted in the world, of subduing be-
setting sins, and of " not thinking of our-
" selves more highly than we ought." The
acquisition of glory was the precept of other

religions, the *contempt* of it is the perfection of Christianity.

Let us then be consistent, and we shall never be contemptible, even in the eyes of our enemies. Let not the unbeliever say that we have one set of opinions for our theory, and another for our practice; that to the vulgar

> We shew the rough and thorny way to heav'n,
> While we the primrose path of dalliance tread.

Would it not become the character of a man of sense, of which consistency is a most unequivocal proof, to choose some rule and abide by it? An extempore Christian is a ridiculous character. Fixed principles, if they be really principles of the heart, and not merely opinions of the understanding, will be followed by a consistent course of action; while indecision of spirit will produce instability of conduct. If there be a model which we profess to admire, let us square our lives by it. If either the Koran of Mahomet, or the Revelations of Zoroaster, be a perfect guide, let us follow one of them. If either Epicurus, Zeno, or Confucius, be the peculiar object of our veneration and respect, let us. avowedly fashion our conduct by the dictates of their philosophy; and then, though we may be wrong, we shall not be absurd; we may be erroneous, but we shall not be inconsistent; but if the Bible be in truth the word of God, as we profess to believe, we need look no farther for a consummate pattern. " If the Lord be God, let us follow HIM." If Christ be a sacrifice for sin, let Him be also to us the example of an holy life.

But I am willing to flatter myself that the moral and intellectual scene about us begins to brighten. I indulge myself in moments of the most enthusiastic and delightful vision, that things are beginning gradually to lead to the fulfilment of that promise, that " all the kingdoms of the " earth shall become the kingdoms of our " God and of his Christ." I take encouragement that that glorious prophecy, that " of the increase of his government " there shall be no end," seems to be gradually accomplishing; and in no instance more, perhaps, than in the noble attempt about to be made for the abolition of the African Slave-trade.* For what event can human wisdom foresee more likely to contribute to " give the Son the Heathen " for his inheritance, and the uttermost " parts of the earth for his possession," than the success of such an enterprise, which will restore the lustre of the British name, and cut off at a single stroke as large and disgraceful a portion of national guilt as ever impaired the virtue, or dishonoured the councils of a Christian country.

A good spirit seems to be at work. A catholic temper is diffusing itself among all . sects and parties: an enlightened candour, and a liberal toleration, were never more prevalent; good men combat each other's

* This interesting question was then beginning to be agitated in parliament. The struggle has been long! The event has been glorious!

opinions with less rancour, and better manners ;* they hate each other less for those
points in which they disagree, and love each
other more for those points in which they
join issue than they formerly did. We
have many public encouragements; we have
a pious king; a wise and virtuous minister;
very many respectable, and not a few serious
clergy. Their number I am willing to
hope is daily increasing. Among these
some of the first in dignity are the most
exemplary in conduct. An increasing desire to instruct the poor, to inform the
ignorant, and to reclaim the vicious, is
spreading among us. The late Royal Proclamation affords an honourable sanction to
virtuous endeavours, and lends nerves and
sinews to the otherwise feeble exertions of
individuals, by enforcing laws wisely plan-
ned, but hitherto feebly executed. In
short, there is a good hope that we shall
more and more become " that happy peo-
" ple who have the Lord for their God :"

* This was written before the French Revolution !!!

that as prosperity is already within our walls peace and virtue may abide in our dwellings.

But vain will be all endeavours after *partial* and *subordinate* amendment. Reformation must begin with the GREAT, or it will never be effectual. *Their* example is the fountain whence the vulgar draw their habits, actions, and characters. To expect to reform the poor while the opulent are corrupt, is to throw odours into the stream while the springs are poisoned.

If, therefore, the Rich and Great will not, from a liberal spirit of doing right, and from a Christian spirit of fearing God, abstain from those offences, for which the poor are to suffer fines and imprisonments, effectual good cannot be done. It will signify little to lay penalties on the horses of the drover, or on the waggon of the husbandman, while the chariot wheels of the great roll with incessant motion; and while the sacred day on which the sons of industry are commanded by royal proclamation to desist from travelling, is for that very reason selected for the journeys of the

Great, and preferred, because the road is encumbered with fewer interruptions. But will it not strike every well-meaning Sunday traveller with a generous remorse, when he reflects that he owes the accommodation of an unobstructed road to the very obedience which is paid by others to that divine and human law which he is in the very act of violating?

Will not the common people think it a little inequitable that they are abridged of the diversions of the public-house and the gaming-yard on Sunday evening, when they shall hear that many houses of the first nobility are on that evening crowded with company, and such amusements carried on as are prohibited by human laws even on common days? As imitation, and a desire of being in the fashion, govern the lower orders of mankind, it is to be feared that they will not think reformation reputable, while they see it *recommended* only, and not *practised*, by their superiors. A precept counteracted by an example, is worse than

fruitless, it is ridiculous : and the common
people will be tempted to set an inferior
value on goodness, when they find it is only
expected from the lower ranks. They cannot surely but smile at the disinterestedness
of their superiors, who, while they seem
anxiously concerned to save others, are so
little solicitous about their own state. The
ambitious vulgar will hardly relish a salvation which is only intended for plebeians ;
nor will they be apt to entertain very exalted notions of that promised future reward,
the road to which they perceive their betters
are so much more earnest to point out to
them, than to walk in themselves.

It was not by inflicting pains and penalties
that Christianity first made its way into the
world : the divine truths it inculcated received irresistible confirmation from the
Lives, Practices, and Examples of its
venerable professors. These were arguments which no popular prejudice could
resist, no Jewish logic refute, and no Pagan
persecution discredit. Had the primitive

Christians only *praised and promulgated* the
most perfect religion the world ever saw, it
would have produced but very slender
effects on the faith and manners of the
people, The astonishing consequences
which followed the pure doctrines of the
Gospel, would never have been produced
if the jealous and inquisitive eye of malice
could have detected that the DOCTRINES
the Christians recommended had not been
illustrated by the LIVES they led.

POSTSCRIPT

———

THE public favour having already brought this little Essay to another Edition, the Author has been sedulous to discover any particular objections that have been made to it. Since the preceding sheets were printed off, it has been suggested by some very respectable persons who have honoured this slight performance with their notice, that it inculcates a too rigid austerity, and carries the point of observing Sunday much too far; that it takes away all the usual occupations of the day, without substituting any others in their stead; and that it only pulls down a wrong system, without so much as attempting to build up a right one. To these observations the Author begs leave to reply, that whilst

animadverting on error, the insisting on obvious duty was purposely omitted. To tell
people what they already know to be right,
was less the intention of this address, than
to observe upon practices which long habit
had prevented them from perceiving to be
wrong. Sensible and well-meaning persons can hardly be at a loss on a subject
which has exhausted precept and wearied
exhortation. To have expatiated on it,
would only have been to repeat what is
already known and acknowledged to be
right, even by those whom the hurry of engagements will not allow to take breath one
day in a week, that they may run the race
of pleasure with more alacrity on the other
six. But probably it is not the duties, but
the amusements appropriated to the day
about which the enquiry is made. It will,
perhaps, be found, that the intervals of a
Sunday regularly devoted to all its reasonable and obvious employments, are not
likely to be so very tedious, but that they
might be easily and pleasantly filled up by

cheerful, innocent, and instructive conversation. Human delights would be very
circumscribed indeed if the practices
here noticed as erroneous, included the
whole circle of enjoyment. In addition
to the appropriate pleasures of devotion,
are the pleasures of retirement, the pleasures
of friendship, the pleasures of intellect,
and the pleasures of beneficence, to be
estimated as nothing?

There will not be found, perhaps, a
single person who shall honour these pages
with a perusal, who has not been repeatedly
told, with an air of imposing gravity,
by those who produce cards on a Sunday
evening, *that it is better to play than to talk
scandal*. Before this pithy axiom was in-
vented, it was not perhaps suspected that
Sunday gaming would ever be adduced as
an argument in favour of morals. Without entering into the comparative excellence
of these two occupations, or presuming to
determine which has a claim to pre-eminence
of piety, may we not venture to be thankful

that these alternatives do not seem to empty
the whole stock of human resource; but
that something will still be left to occupy
and to interest those who adopt neither the
one nor the other?

People in the gay and elegant scenes of
life are perpetually complaining that an extensive acquaintance, and the necessity of
being constantly engaged in large circles
and mixed assemblies, leaves them little
leisure for family enjoyment, select conversation, and domestic delights. Others,
with no less earnestness, lament that the
hurry of public stations, and the necessary
demands of active life, allow them no time.
for any but frivolous reading. Now the
recurrence of one Sunday in every week
seems to hold out an inviting remedy for
both these evils. The sweet and delightful
pleasures of family society might then be
uninterruptedly enjoyed, by the habitual
exclusion of trifling and idle visitors, who
do not come to see their friends, but to get
rid of themselves. Persons of fashion

living in the same house, and connected by the closest ties, whom business and pleasure keep asunder during the greatest part of the week, would then have an opportunity of spending a little time together, and of cultivating that friendship for each other, that affection for their children, and that intercourse with their Maker, to which the present manners are not *very* favourable. To the other set of complainers, those who can find no time to read, this interval naturally presents itself; and it so happens, that some of the most enlightened men the world ever saw have, not unfrequently, devoted their rare talents to subjects peculiarly suited to this day; and that not merely in the didactic form of sermons, which men of the world affect to disdain; but in every alluring shape which human ingenuity could assume. It can be fortunately produced among a thousand other instances, that the deepest metaphysician,* the greatest astro-

* Locke, Newton, Milton, Butler, Addison, Bacon, Boyle.

nomer, the sublimest poet, the acutest rea-
soner, the politest writer, the most consummate philospher, and the profoundest
investigator of nature, which this, or perhaps any country has produced, have all
written on such subjects as are analogous
to the business of the Lord's day. Such
authors as these, even wits, philosophers,
and men of the world, must acknowledge
that it is not bigotry to read, nor enthusiasm to commend. Of this illustrious
groupe only *one* was a clergyman, which to
a certain class of readers will be a strong
recommendation: though it is a little hard
that the fastidiousness of modern taste
should undervalue the learned and pious
labours of divines, only because they are
professional. In every other function, a
man's compositions are not the less esteemed
because they peculiarly belong to his more
immediate business. Blackstone's opinions
in jurisprudence are in high reputation,
though he was a lawyer: Sydenham is still
consulted as oracular in fevers, in spite of

his having been a physician; and the Commentaries of Cæsar are of established authority in military operations, notwithstanding he was a soldier.

ESTIMATE

OF THE

RELIGION

OF THE

FASHIONABLE WORLD.

There was never found in any age of the world, either Philosophy, or Sect, or Religion, or Law, or Dicipline, which
did so highly exalt the public good as the Christian Faith.

LORD BACON.

CONTENTS.

CHAPTER I.

Decline of Christianity shewn, by a comparative
View of the Religion of the Great in preceding
Ages   :   -   •   -   111

CHAPTER II.

Benevolence allowed to be the reigning Virtue,
but not *exclusively* the Virtue of the present
Age.—Benevolence not the whole of Religion,
though one of its most characteristic Features.
Whether Benevolence proceed from a religious
Principle will be more infalliable known by the
general Disposition of Time, Fortune, and the
common Habits of Life, than from a few occasional Acts of Bounty   -   -   123

CHAPTER III.

The Neglect of Religious Education both a Cause
and Consequence of the Decline of Christianity.
—No Moral Restraints.—Religion only incidentally taught, not as a Principle of Action.—
A few of the many Causes which dispose the
Young to entertain low Opinions of Religion   -   -   -   139

CHAPTER IV.

Other Symptoms of the Decline of Christianity.—
No Family Religion.—Corrupt or negligent Example of Superiors.—The self-denying and evangelical Virtues held in contempt.—Neglect of
encouraging and promoting Religion among
Servants   -   -   -   - 177

CHAPTER V.

The negligent Conduct of Christians, no real Objection against Christianity.— The Reason why
its Effects are not more manifest to worldly
Men, is, because Believers do not lead Christian
Lives.—Professors differ but little in their Practice
from Unbelievers.—Even real Christians are too
diffident and timid, and afraid of acting up to
their Principles.—The Absurdity of the Charge
commonly brought against Serious People, that
they are too strict.   -   -   202

CHAPTER VI.

A Stranger, from observing the Fashionable Mode of Life, would not take this to be a Christian Country.—Lives of professing Christians examined by a Comparison with the Gospel.—Christianity not made the Rule of Life, even by those who profess to receive it as an Object of Faith.—Temporizing Writers contribute to lower the Credit of Christianity—Loose Harangues on Morals not calculated to reform the Heart. - - - - - 236

CHAPTER VII.

View of those who acknowledge Christianity as a perfect System of Morals, but deny its Divine Authority.—Morality not the whole of Religion - - - - 251 that Christianity, like its Divine Author, is not only *denied* by those who in so many words disown their submission to its authority, but is *betrayed* by the still more treacherous disciple, even while he cries, *Hail, Master!*

For this visible declension of piety various reasons have been assigned, some of which however do not seem fully adequate to the effects ascribed to them. The author of a late popular pamphlet* has accounted for the increased profligacy of the *common people*, by ascribing it, very justly, to the increased dissoluteness of their superiors. And who will deny what he farther affirms ——that the general conduct of high and low receives a deep tincture of depravity from the growing neglect of public worship? So far I most cordially agree with the noble author. Nothing can be more obvious, than that the disuse of public worship is

---

* Hints to an Association for preventing Vice and Immorality, written by a Nobleman of the highest rank.

naturally followed by a neglect of all religious duties. Energies, which are not called out into action, almost necessarily die in the mind. The soul, no less than the body, requires its stated repairs, and regular renovations. And from the sluggish and procrastinating spirit of man, that religious duty to which no fixed time is assigned, is seldom, it is to be feared, performed at all.*

I must, however, take leave to dissent from the opinion of the noble author, that the too common desertion of persons of rank from the service of the establishment is occasioned in general, as he intimates, by their disapprobation of the Liturgy; as it may more probably be supposed, that the far greater part of them are deterred from going to church by motives widely removed from speculative objections and conscientious scruples.

It would be quite foreign to my present

* On this Subject see Dr. Johnson's Life of Milton.

purpose to enter upon the question of the superior utility of a form of prayer for public worship. Most sincerely attached to the establishment myself, not, as far as I am able to judge, from prejudice, but from a fixed and settled conviction; I regard its institutions with a veneration at once affectionate and rational. Never need a Christian, except when his own heart is strangely indisposed, fail to derive benefit from its ordinances, and he may bless the overruling providence of God, that, in this instance, the natural variableness and inconstancy of human opinion is, as it were, fixed, and settled, and hedged in, by a stated service so pure, so evangelical, and which is enriched by such a large infusion of sacred Scripture.

If so many among us contemn the service as having been, individually, to *us* fruitless and unprofitable, let us inquire whether the blessing may not be withheld because we are not fervent in asking it. —If we do not find a suitable humiliation in the *Con-*

fession, a becoming earnestness in the *Peti-tions*, a congenial joy in the *Adoration*, a corresponding gratitude in the *Thanks-givings*, it is because our hearts do not accompany our words; it is because we rest in " the form of godliness," and are con-tented to remain destitute of its " power." If we are not duly interested when the select portions of Scripture are read to us, it is because we do not as " new-born babes " desire the sincere milk of the word, that " we may grow thereby."

Perhaps there has not been since the age of the Apostles, a church upon earth, in which the public worship was so solemn and so cheerful; so simple, yet so sublime; so full of fervour, at the same time so free from enthusiasm; so rich in the gold of Christian antiquity, yet so astonishingly exempt from its dross. That it has imper-fections, we do not deny; but what are they compared with its general excellence? They are as the spots on the sun's disk, which a sharp observer may detect, but which neither diminish the warmth, nor obscure the brightness.

But if those imperfections which are inseparable from all human institutions, are to be alleged as reasons for abstaining to attend on the service of the established church; we must, on the same principle, and on still stronger grounds, abstain from all public worship whatever; and indeed it must be confessed, that the persons of whom we are now speaking, are very consistent in this matter.

But the difference of opinion from that of the noble author here intimated, is not so much about the Liturgy itself, as the imaginary effects attributed to it in thinning the pews of our people of fashion. The slightest degree of observation serves to contradict this assertion. Those however, who, with the noble author, maintain the other opinion, may satisfy their doubts by inquiring, whether the regular and systematic absentees from church are chiefly to be found among the thinking, the reading, the speculative, and the scrupulous part of mankind.

Even the most negligent attendant on public worship must know, that the obnoxious creed, to whose malignant potency this general desertion is ascribed by the noble author, is never read above three or four Sundays in the year; and even allowing the validity of the objections brought against it, that does not seem a very adequate reason for banishing the most scrupulous and tender consciences from church on the remaining eight-and-forty Sundays of the calendar.

Besides, there is one test which is absolutely unequivocal: this creed is never read at all in the afternoon, any more than the Litany, that other great source of offence and supposed desertion; and yet, with all these multiplied reasons for their attendance, do we see the conscientious crowds of the high-born, who abstain from the morning service through their repugnance to subscribe to the dogmas of Athanasius, or the

more orthodox clauses of the morning
Litany ; do we see them, I say, flocking to
the evening service, impatient for the exercise of that devotion which had been
obstructed by these two objectionable portions of the Liturgy? Do we see them
eager to explain the cause of their morning absence, and zealous to vindicate their
piety by assiduously attending when the
reprobated portions of divine service are
omitted? So far from it, is it not pretty
evident that the general quarrel (with some
few exceptions) of those who habitually
absent themselves from public worship, is
not with the Creed, but the Commandments?
With such, to reform the Prayer-Book
would go but a little way, unless the New
Testament could be also abridged. Cut,
and pare, and prune the service of the
Church ever so much, still that Christianity
itself, which is its ground-work, will be
found full of formidable objections. Should
the Church even give up her abstruse
creeds, it would avail but little, unless

the Bible would also expunge those rigorous
laws which not only prohibit sinful actions,
but corrupt inclinations.   And to speak
honestly, I do not see how such persons
as habitually infringe the laws of virtue
and sobriety, and who yet are men of
acute sagacity, accustomed on other subjects to a consistent train of reasoning ; who
see consequences . in their causes ; who
behold practical self-denial necessarily
involved in the sincere habit of religious
observances—I do not see how, with respect
to such men, any doctrines reformed, any
redundances lopped, any obscurities brightened, could effect the object of the noble
author's very benevolent and christian
wish.

Religious duties are often neglected upon
more consistent grounds than the friends of
religion are willing to allow.   They are
often discontinued, not as repugnant to the
understanding, not as repulsive to the judgment, but as hostile to a worldly, as
well as, licentious life. And when a

prudent man, after having entered into a
solemn convention, finds that he is living
in a constant breach of every article of the
treaty he has engaged to observe, one cannot much wonder at his getting out of the
hearing of the heavy artillery which he
knows is planted against him, and against
every one who lives in the allowed infrac-
tion of the covenant into which every
Christian has solemnly entered.

For is it not obvious, that a man of
sense who should acknowledge the truth of
the doctrine, would find himself obliged
to submit to the force of the precept? It
is not easy to be a comfortable sinner,
without trying, at least, to be a confirmed
unbeliever. And as that cannot be achieved
by a wish, the next expedient is to shun
the recollection of that belief, and to forget that of which we cannot be ignorant.
The smallest remains of faith would
embitter a life of libertinism, and to be
frequently reminded of the articles of that
faith would disturb the ease induced by a

neglect of all observances. While to such a one who retains any impression of Christianity, the wildest festivals of intemperance will be converted into the terrifying feast of Damocles.

That many a respectable non-conformist is kept out of the pale of the establishment by some of the causes noticed by the noble author, cannot be questioned, and a just matter of regret it is. But these, however, are often sober thinkers, serious inquirers, conscientious reasoners, whose object we may charitably believe is truth, however they may be deceived as to its nature: but that the same objections banish the great and the gay is not equally evident. Thanks to the indolence and indifference of the times; it is not dogmas or doctrines, it is not abstract reasonings, or puzzling propositions, it is not perplexed argument, or intricate metaphysics, which can now disincline from Christianity; so far from it, they cannot even allure to unbelief. Infidelity itself, with all that strong and natural bias which selfishness and appetite entertain in its favour, if it appear in the grave and scholastic form of speculation, argument, or philosophical deduction, may now lie almost as quietly on the shelf as the volumes of its most able antagonist; and the cobwebs are almost as seldom brushed from Hobbes as from Hooker. No: prudent scepticism has wisely studied the temper of the times, and skilfully felt the pulse of this relaxed, and indolent, and selfish age. It prudently accommodated itself to the reigning character, when it adopted sarcasm instead of reasoning, and preferred a sneer to an argument. It discreetly judged, that, if it would now gain proselytes, it must shew itself under the bewitching form of a profane bon-mot; must be interwoven in the texture of some amusing history, written with the levity of a romance, and the point and glitter of an epigram: it must embellish the ample margin with some offensive anecdote or impure allusion, and decorate impiety with every loose and meretricious ornament which a corrupt imagination can invent. It must break up the old flimsy system into little mischievous aphorisms, ready for practical purposes: it must divide the rope of sand into little portable parcels, which the shallowest wit can comprehend, and the shortest memory carry away.

Philosophy therefore (as Unbelief, by a patent of its own creation, has lately been pleased to call itself) will not do nearly so much mischief to the present age as its primitive apostles intended: since it requires time, application, and patience to peruse the reasoning-veterans of the sceptic school: and time, and application, and patience, are talents not now very severely devoted to study of any sort, by those who give the law to fashion; especially since, as it was hinted above, the same principles may be acquired on cheaper terms, and the reputation of being philosophers obtained without the sacrifice of pleasure for the severities of study; since the industry of our literary chemists has extracted the spirit from the gross substance of the old unvendible poison, and exhibited it in the volatile essence of a few sprightly sayings.

If therefore, in this voluptuous age, when a frivolous and relaxing dissipation has infected our very studies, infidelity will not be at the pains of deep research and elaborate investigation, even on such subjects as are congenial to its affections, and promotive of its object; it is vain to expect that Christianity will be more engaging, either as an object of speculation, or as a rule of practice; since it demands a still stronger exertion of those energies which the gay world is not at the pains to exercise, even on the side they approve. For the evidences of Christianity require attention to be comprehended, no less than its doctrines require humility to be received, and its precepts self-denial to be obeyed.

Will it then be uncharitable to pronounce, that the leading mischief—not which thins our churches—for that is not the evil I propose to consider—but which pervades our whole character, and gives the colour to our general conduct, is *practical irreligion?* an irreligion not so much opposed to a speculative faith, not so much in hostility to the evidences of christianity, as to that spirit, temper, and behaviour which christianity inculcates.

On this practical irreligion it is proposed to offer a few hints. After attempting to shew, by a comparison with the religion of the great in preceding ages, that there is a visible decline of piety among the higher ranks—that even those more liberal spirits who neglect not many of the great duties of benevolence, yet hold the severer obligations of piety in no esteem—I shall proceed, though perhaps with too little method, to remark on the notorious *effects* of the decay of this religious principle, as it corrupts our mode of education, infects domestic conduct, spreads the contagion downwards among servants and inferiors, and influences our general manners, habits, and conversation.

But what it is here proposed principally to insist on is, that this defect of religious principle is almost equally fatal, as to all

the ends and purposes of genuine piety,
whether it appear in the open contempt
and defiance of all sacred institutions, or
whether it shield itself under the more decent veil of external observances, unsup-
ported by such a conduct as is analogous
to the christian profession.

I shall proceed with a few remarks on a
third class of fashionable characters, who
profess to acknowledge christianity as a
perfect system of morals, while they deny
its divine authority : and conclude with
some slight animadversions on the opinion
which these modish christians maintain,
that morality is the whole of religion.

It must be confessed, however, that
manners and principles act reciprocally on
each other; and are, by turns, cause, and
effect. For instance—the increased relaxa-
tion of morals produces the increased neglect of infusing religious principles in the
education of youth : which effect becomes,
in its turn, a cause; and in due time,
when that cause comes to operate, helps on
the decline of manners.

CHAPTER I.

Decline of Christianity shewn, by a compara-
tive View of the Religion of the Great in
preceding Ages.

IF the general position of this little tract be
allowed, namely, that religion is at present
in no very flourishing state among those
whose example, from the high ground on
which they stand, guides and governs the
rest of mankind, it will not be denied by
those who are ever so superficially acquainted with the history of our country, that
this has not always been the case. Those
who are able to make a fair comparison
must allow, that however the present age
may be improved in other important and
valuable advantages, yet that there is but
little appearance remaining among the great
and the powerful of that " righteousness
which exalteth a nation;"—They must
confess that there has been a *moral revolu-*

tion in the national manners and principles, very little analogous to that great
political one which we hear so much and
so justly extolled. That our public virtue
bears little proportion to our public blessings; and that our religion has decreased
in a pretty exact proportion to our having
secured the means of enjoying it.

That the antipodes to wrong are hardly
ever right, was very strikingly illustrated
about the middle of the last century, when
the fiery and indiscreet zeal of one party
was made a pretext for the profligate impiety of the other; who, to the bad principle which dictated a depraved conduct,
added the bad taste of being proud of it :—
when even the least abandoned were ab-
surdly apprehensive that an appearance of
decency might subject them to the charge
of fanaticism, a charge in which they took
care to involve real piety as well as enthusiastic pretence, till it became the general
fashion to avoid no sin but hypocrisy, to
dread no imputation but that of seriousness,

and to be more afraid of the virtues which
procure a good reputation than of every vice
which ever earned a bad one. Party was
no longer confined to political distinctions,
but became a part of morals, and was
carried into religion itself. The more
profligate of the court party began to con-
nect the idea of devotion with that of
republicanism; and to prove their aversion
to the one, thought they could never cast too
much ridicule upon the other. The public
taste became debauched; to be licentious in
principle, was thought by many to be the
best way of making their court to the
restored Monarch; open corruption was
adopted by way of proving their abhorrence of the hypocritical side; and *Poems
by a person of honour*, the phrase of the day
to designate a fashionable author, were
often scandalous offences against modesty
and virtue.

It was not till piety was thus unfortu-
nately brought into disrepute, that persons
of condition thought it made their sincerity,

their abilities, or their good breeding questionable, to appear openly on the side of religion. A strict attachment to piety did not subtract from a great reputation. Men were not thought the worse lawyers, generals, ministers, legislators, or histo- rians, for believing, and even defending, the religion of their country. The gallant Sir Philip Sidney, the rash but heroic Essex, the politic and sagacious Burleigh, the all- accomplished Falkland,* not only publicly owned their belief in christianity, but even wrote some things of a religious nature.†
These instances, and many others which might be aduced, are not, it will be allowed, selected from among contemplative recluses, grave divines, or authors by profession; but from the busy, the active, and the illus- trious; from public characters, from men of

* Lord Falkland assisted the great Chillingworth in his incomparable work, The Religion of a Pro- testant.

† See that equally elegant and authentic work, *The Anecdotes of Royal and Noble Authors.*

strong passions, beset with great temptations; distinguished actors on the stage of
life; and whose respective claims to the
title of fine gentlemen, brave soldiers, or
able statesmen, have never been called in
question.

What would the Hales, and the Claren-
dons, and the Somerses* have said, had
they been told that the time was at no
great distance when that sacred book, for
which they thought it no derogation from
their wisdom or their dignity to entertain
the profoundest reverence; the book which
they made the rule of their faith, the
object of their most serious study, and
the foundation of their eternal hope; that
this book would one day be of little more
use to men in high public stations, than to
be the instrument of an oath; and that the

---

* This consummate statesman was not only remarkable for a strict attendance on the public duties
of religion, but for maintaining them with equal exactness in his family, at a period too when religion
was most discountenanced.

sublimest rites of the christian religion would soon be considered as little more than a necessary qualification for a place, or the legal preliminary to an office?

This indeed is the boasted period of free enquiry and liberty of thinking. But it is the peculiar character of the present age, that its mischiefs often assume the most alluring forms; and that the most alarming evils not only look so like goodness as to be often mistaken for it, but are sometimes mixed up with so much real good, as often to disguise, though never to counteract, their malignity. Under the beautiful mask of an enlightened philosophy, all religious restraints are set at nought; and some of the deadliest wounds have been aimed at christianity, in works written in avowed vindication of the most amiable of all the christian principles.* Even the prevalence

* See particularly *Voltaire sur la Tolerance.* This is a common artifice of that insidious author. In this instance he has made use of the popularity he obtained in the fanatical tragedy at Thoulouse, (the

of a liberal and warm philanthropy is se-
cretly sapping the foundation of christian
morals, because many of its champions allow themselves to live in the open violation
of the severer duties of justice and sobriety,
while they are contending for the gentler
ones of charity and beneficence.

The strong and generous bias in favour
of universal toleration, noble as the principle itself is, has engendered a dangerous
notion that all error is innocent. Whether
it be owing to this or to whatever other
cause, it is certain that the discriminating
features of the christian religion are every
day growing into less repute; and it is
become the fashion even among the better

murder of Calas) to discredit, though in the most
guarded manner, christianity itself; degrading mar-
tyrdoms, denying the truth of the Pagan persecu-
tions, &c. &c. And by mixing some truths with
many falsehoods, by assuming an amiable candour,
and professing to serve the interest of goodness, he
treacherously contrives to leave on the mind of the un-
guarded reader impressions the most unfavourable to
christianity.

'sort, to evade, to lower, or to generalize, its most distinguishing peculiarities.

There is so little of the Author of christianity left in his own religion, that an apprehensive believer is ready to exclaim with the woman at the sepulchre, " They " have taken away my Lord, and I know " not where they have laid him." The locality of Hell and the existence of an Evil Spirit are annihilated, or considered as abstract ideas, as Metaphors, as Allegories. When they are alluded to, it is periphrastically. · They are discontinued not on the ground of their being awful and terrible, but they are set aside as topics too vulgar for the polished, too illiberal for the learned, and as savouring too much of credulity for the enlightened.

While we justly glory in having freed ourselves from the trammels of human authority, are we not turning our liberty into licentiousness, and wantonly struggling to throw off the *divine* authority too? Freedom of thought is the glory of the human

mind ; while it is confined within its just
and sober limits ; but though we may think
ourselves accountable for *opinions* at no
earthly tribunal, yet it should be remembered, that thoughts as well as actions are
amenable at the bar of God.   Though
we may rejoice that the tyranny of the
spiritual Procrustes is so far annihilated,
that we are in no danger of having our
opinions lopped or lengthened till they are
brought to fit the measure of human ca-
price, yet there is still a standard by
which not only actions are weighed, but
opinions are judged ; and every sentiment
which is clearly inconsistent with the revealed will of God, is as much throwing
off *his* dominion as the breach of any of his
moral precepts.   This cuts up by the
roots that popular and independent phrase,
that " thoughts are free ;" for in this view
we are no more at liberty to indulge
opinions in opposition to the express
word of God than we are at liberty to infringe practically on his commandments.

There is then surely one test by which it is no mark of intolerance to try the principles of men, namely, the *Law and the Testimony* : and on applying to this touchstone, it is impossible not to lament, that, while a more generous spirit governs our judgment, a purer principle does not seem to regulate our lives. May it not be said, that, while we are justly commended for thinking charitably of the opinions of others, we seem, in return, as if we were desirous of furnishing them with an opportunity of exercising their candour by the laxity of principle in which we indulge ourselves? If the hearts of men were as firmly united to each other by the bond of charity as some pretend, they could not fail of being united to God also by one common principle of piety. For christian piety furnishes the only certain sourse of all charitable judgment, as well as of all virtuous conduct.

Instead of abiding by the salutary precept

of *judging no man*, it is the fashion to exceed our commission, and to fancy every body to be in a safe state. " Judge not" is the precise limit of our rule. This rule furnishes no more encouragement to judge falsely on the side of worldly candour, than to judge harshly on the side of Christian charity. In forming our notions we have to chuse between the bible and the world, between the rule and the practice. Where these do not agree, it is left to the judgment of believers, at least, by which we are to decide. But we never act, in religious concerns, by the same rule of common sense and equitable judgment which governs us on other occasions. In weighing any commodity, its weight is determined by some generally allowed standard; and if the commodity be heavier or lighter than the standard weight, we add to or take from it : but we never break, or clip, or reduce the weight to suit the thing we are weighing; because the common consent of mankind has agreed that the one shall be considered as the standard to ascertain the value of the other. But, in weighing our principles by the standard of the Gospel, we do just the reverse. Instead of bringing our opinions and actions to the *balance of the sanctuary* in order to determine and rectify their comparative deficiencies, we lower and reduce the standard of the scripture doctrines till we have accomodated them to our own purposes : so that, instead of trying others and ourselves by God's unerring rule, we invert the order of things, we try the truth of God's rule by its conformity or non-conformity to our own depraved notions and corrupt practices.

CHAPTER II.

Benevolence allowed to be the reigning Virtue, but not exclusively the Virtue of the present Age.—Benevolence not the whole of Religion, though one of its most characteristic Features. Whether Benevolence proceeds from a Religious Principle, will be more infallibly known by the general Disposition of Time, Fortune, and the common Habits of Life, than from a few occasional Acts of Bounty.

To all the remonstrance and invective of the preceding chapter, there will not fail to be opposed that which we hear every day so loudly insisted on,—the decided superiority of the present age in other and better respects. It will be said, that even those who neglect the outward forms of religion, exhibit however the best proofs of the best principles; that the unparalleled instances of charity of which we are continual witnesses; that the many striking acts of public bounty, and the various new and noble improvements in this shining virtue, justly entitle the present age to be called, by way of eminence, *the age of benevolence.*

It is with the liveliest joy I acknowledge the delightful truth. Liberality flows with a full tide through a thousand channels. There is scarcely a newspaper but records some meeting of men of fortune for the most salutary purposes. The noble and numberless structures for the relief of distress, which are the ornament and the glory of our metropolis, proclaim a species of munificence unknown to former ages. Subscriptions, not only to hospitals, but to various other valuable institutions, are obtained almost as soon as solicited. And who but must wish that these beautiful monuments of benevolence may become every day more numerous, and more extended!

Yet, with all these allowed and obvious excellencies, it is not quite clear whether something too much has not been said of the liberality of the present age, in a com-

parative view with that of those ages which
preceded it. A general alteration of habits
and manners has at the same time multiplied public bounties and private distress;
and it is scarcely a paradox, to say that
there was probably less misery when there
was less munificence.

If an increased benevolence now ranges
through, and relieves a wider compass of
distress ; yet still, if those examples of luxury and dissipation which promote that distress are still *more* increased, this makes the
good done bear little proportion to the evil
promoted. If the miseries *removed* by the
growth of charity fall, both in number
and weight, far below those which are
caused by the growth of vice and disorder;
if we find that, though bounty is extended,
yet those corruptions which make bounty
so necessary are extended also, almost beyond calculation; if it appear that, though
more objects are relieved by our money,
yet incomparably more are debauched by
our licentious habits—the balance perhaps

will not turn out so decidedly in favour of the times as we are willing to imagine.

If then the most valuable species of charity is that which prevents distress by preventing or lessening vice, the greatest and most inevitable cause of want,—we ought not so highly to exalt the bounty of the great in the present day, in preference to that broad shade of protection, patronage, and maintenance, which the wide-spread bounty of their forefathers stretched out over whole villages, I had almost said whole provinces. When a few noblemen in a county, like their own stately oaks (paternal oaks! which were not often set upon a card) extended their sheltering branches to shield all the underwood of the forest—when there existed a kind of passive charity, a negative sort of benevolence, which did good of itself; and without effort, exertion, or expence, produced the effect of all, and performed the best functions of bounty, though it did not aspire to the dignity of its name—it was simply this:—*great people*

staid at home ; and the sober pomp and orderly magnificence of a noble family, residing
at their own castle great part of the year,
contributed in the most natural way to the
maintenance of the poor, by employing
them; and in a good degree *prevented* that
distress, which it must however thankfully
be confessed it is the laudable object of modern bounty to *relieve*. A man of fortune
might not then, it is true, so often dine in
public for the benefit of the poor ; but the
poor were more regularly and comfortably
fed with the abundant crumbs which then
fell from the rich man's table. Whereas it
cannot be denied that the prevailing mode
of living has pared real hospitality to the
very quick; and, though the remark may
be thought ridiculous, it is a material dis-
advantage to the poor that the introduction
of the modern unsubstantial style of luxury
has rendered the remains of the most costly
table but of small value.

But even allowing the boasted superiority
of modern benevolence, still it will not be

inconsistent with the object of the present design, to enquire whether the diffusion of this branch of charity, though the most lovely offspring of religion, be yet any positive proof of the prevalence of religious principle? and whether it be not the fashion rather to consider Benevolence as a substitute for Christianity than as an evidence of it?

It seems to be one of the reigning errors among the better sort, to reduce all religion into benevolence, and all benevolence into alms-giving. The wide and comprehensive idea of Christian charity is compressed into the slender compass of a little pecuniary relief. This species of benevolence is indeed a bright gem among the ornaments of a Christian; but by no means furnishes all the jewels of his crown, which derives its lustre from the associated radiance of every christian grace. Besides, the genuine virtues are all of the same family; and it is only by being seen in company with each other, and with Piety their common parent, that they are certainly known to be legitimate.

But it is the property of the *christian* virtues, that, like all other amiable members of the same family, while each is doing its own particular duty, it is contributing to the prosperity of the rest; and the larger the family, the better they live together, as no one can advance itself, without labouring for the advancement of the whole: thus, no man can be benevolent on christian principles without self-denial; and so of the other virtues: each is connected with some other, and all with religion.

I already anticipate the obvious and hackneyed reply, that " whoever be the instru " ment, and whatever be the motive of " bounty, still the poor are equally relieved, " and therefore the end is the same." And it must be confessed that those compassionate hearts, who cannot but be earnestly anxious that the distressed should be relieved at any rate, should not too scrupulously enquire in the case of others, into any cause, of which the effect is so beneficial. Nor indeed will candour scrutinize

K

too curiously into the lesser errors of
any life of which benevolence will always
be allowed to be the shining ornament,
while it does not pretend to be the atoning
virtue.

Let me not be misrepresented, as if I
were seeking to detract from the value of
this amiable feeling; we do not surely
lower the practice by seeking to ennoble
the principle; the action will not be impaired by mending the motive : and no one
will be likely to give the poor less because
he seeks to please God more.

· One cannot then help wishing that pecuniary bounty were not only not practised,
but that it were not sometimes enjoined too,
as a redeeming virtue. In many conversations (I had almost said in many charity
sermons) it is insinuated as if a little alms-
giving could pay off old scores contracted
by favourite indulgences. This, though
often done by well-meaning men to advance the interests of some present pious
purpose, yet has the mischievous effect of

those medicines which, while they may relieve a local complaint, are yet undermining the general habit.

That great numbers who are not influenced by so high a principle as Christianity holds out, are yet truly compassionate without hypocrisy and without ostentation, who can doubt? But who that feels the beauty of benevolence can avoid being solicitous, not only that its offerings should comfort the receiver, but return in blessings to the bosom of the giver, by springing from such motives, and being accompanied by such a temper as shall redound to his eternal good! For that the benefit is the same to the object, whatever be the character of the benefactor, is but an uncomfortable view of things to a real Christian, whose compassion reaches to the souls of men. Such a one longs to see the charitable giver as happy himself, as he is endeavouring to make the object of his bounty; but such a one knows that no happiness can be fully and finally enjoyed but on the solid basis of Christian piety.

For as religion is not, on the one hand, merely an opinion or a sentiment, so neither is it, on the other, merely an act or a performance; but it is a disposition, a habit, a temper: it is not a name, but a nature: it is a turning the whole mind to God: it is a concentration of all the powers and affections of the soul into one steady point, an uniform desire to please *Him*. This desire will naturally and necessarily manifest itself in our doing all the good we can to our fellow-creatures in every possible way; for it will be found that neither of the two parts into which practical religion is divided, can be performed with any degree of perfection but by those who unite both: as it may be questioned if any man really *does* " love his neighbour as himself," who does not first endeavour to " love God with all " his heart." As genius has been defined to be strong general powers of mind, accidentally determined to some particular pursuit, so piety may be denominated a strong general disposition of the heart to every thing that is right, breaking forth into every excellent action, as the occasion presents itself. The temper must be ready in the mind, and the whole heart must by its internal principle, be prepared and trained to every act of virtue to which it may be called out. For religious principles are like the military exercise: they keep up an habitual state of preparation for actual service; and, by never relaxing the discipline, the real Christian is ready for every duty to which he may be commanded. Right actions best prove the existence of religion in the heart; but they are evidences, not causes.

Whether therefore a man's charitable actions proceed from religious principle, he will be best able to ascertain by scrutinizing into his own habits of self denial, by marking what is the general disposition of his time and fortune, and by observing whether his pleasures and expences are habitually regulated with a view to enable him to be more or less useful to others.

It is in vain that he possess what is called by the courtesy of fashion *the best heart in the world* (a character we every day hear applied to the libertine and the prodigal) if he squander his time and estate in such a round of extravagant indulgences and thoughtless dissipation as leaves him little money and less leisure for nobler purposes. It makes but little difference whether a man is prevented from doing good by hard-hearted parsimony or an unprincipled extravagance ; the stream of usefulness is equally cut off by both.

The mere *casual* benevolence of any man can have little claim to solid esteem ; nor does any charity deserve the name, which does not grow out of a steady conviction that it is his bounden duty ; which does not spring from a settled propensity to obey the whole will of God ; which is not therefore made a part of the general plan of his conduct ; and which does not lead him to

order the whole scheme of his affairs with
an eye to it.

He therefore who does not habituate
himself to certain interior restraints, who
does not live in a regular course of self-
renunciation, will not be likely often to perform acts of beneficence, when it becomes
necessary to convert to such purposes any of
that time or money which appetite, temptation, or vanity solicits him to divert to
other purposes.

And surely he who seldom sacrifices one
darling indulgence, who does not subtract
one gratification from the incessant round
of his enjoyments, when the indulgence
would obstruct his capacity of doing good,
or when the sacrifice would enlarge his
power, does not deserve the name of *bene-*
volent. And for such an unequivocal criterion of charity, to whom are we to
look but to the conscientious Christian ?
No other spirit but that by which he is go-
verned can subdue self-love: and where
self-love is the predominant passion, bene-

volence can have but a feeble, or an acci-
dental dominion.

Now if we look around, and remark the
excesses of luxury, the costly diversions,
and the intemperate dissipation in which
numbers of professing Christians indulge
themselves, can any stretch of candour, can
even that tender sentiment by which we are
enjoined " to hope" and to " believe all
" things," enable us to hope and believe
that such are actuated by a spirit of Christian
benevolence, merely because we see them
perform some casual acts of charity, which
the spirit of the world can contrive to make
extremely compatible with a voluptuous
life ; and the cost of which, after all, bears
but little proportion to that of any one vice,
or even vanity !

Men will not believe that there is hardly
any one human good quality which will
know and keep its proper bounds, without
the restraining influence of religious principle. There is, for instance, great danger
lest a constant attention to so right a prac-

tice as an invariable œconomy, should
narrow the heart and incline it to the
love of money. Nothing can effectually counteract this natural propensity
but the Christian habit of devoting
those retrenched expences to some good
purpose; and then œconomy, instead of
narrowing the heart, will enlarge it, by inducing a constant association of benevolence
with frugality. An habitual attention to
the wants of others is the only wholesome
regulator of our own expences; and carries
with it a whole train of virtues, disinterestedness, sobriety, and temperance. And those
who live in the custom of levying constant
taxes on their vanities for such purposes,
serve the poor still less than they serve
themselves. For if they are charitable
upon true Christian principles, " they are
" laying up for themselves a good founda-
" tion against the time to come."

Thus when a vein of Christianity runs
through the whole mass of a man's life, it
gives a new value to all his actions, and a

new character to all his views. It trans-
mutes prudence and œconomy into Christian
virtues ; and every offering that is presented
on the altar of charity becómes truly consecrated, when it is the gift of obedience,
and the price of self-deniql. Piety is that fire
from heaven that can alone kindle the sacrifice, which through the mediation and
intercession of our great High Priest " will
" go up for a memorial before God."

On the other hand, when any act of
bounty is performed by way of composition
with our Maker, either as a purchase or
an expiation of unallowed indulgences ;
though, even in this case, God, (who makes
all the passions of men subservient to his
good purposes) can make the gift equally
beneficial to the receiver, yet it is surely
not too severe to say, that to the giver such
acts are an unfounded dependence, a deceitful refuge, a broken staff.

CHAPTER III.

*The Neglect of Religious Education, both a
Cause and a Consequence of the Decline of
Christianity.—No Moral Restraints.—Re-
ligion only incidentally taught, not as a
Principle of Action. A few of the many
Causes which dispose the Young to entertain
low Opinions of Religion.*

LET not the truly pious be offended, as
if, in the present chapter, which is intended
to treat of the notorious neglect of Religious Education, I meant to insinuate
that the principles and tempers of Christianity may be formed in the young mind,
by the mere mechanical operation of early
institution, without the co-operating aid of
the Holy Spirit of God. To imply this
would be indeed to betray a lamentable
ignorance of human nature, of the disorder
that sin has introduced, of the inefficacy of
mere human means; and entirely to mis-

take the genius, and overlook the most obvious and important truths of our holy religion.

It must however be allowed, that the supreme Being works chiefly by means; and though it be confessed that no defect of education, no corruption of manners can place any out of the reach of the Divine influences, (for it is under such circumstances perhaps that some of the most extraordinary instances of Divine grace have been manifested) yet it must be owned, that instructing children in principles of religion, and giving them early habits of temperance and piety, is the way in which we may most confidently expect the Divine blessing. And that it is a work highly pleasing to God, and which will be most assuredly accompanied by his gracious energy, we may judge from what he says of his faithful servant Abraham; " I *know* him that he will " command his children, and his house- " hold after him, and they shall keep the " way of the Lord."

But religion is the only thing in which we seem to look for the end, without making use of the means; and yet it would not be more surprising if we were to expect that our children should become artists and scholars without being bred to arts and languages, than it is to look for a Christian world, without a Christian education.

The noblest objects can yield no delight, if there be not in the mind a disposition to relish them. There must be a congruity between the mind and the object, in order to produce any capacity of enjoyment. To the Mathematician, demonstration is pleasure; to the Philosopher, the study of nature; to the Voluptuary, the gratification of his appetite; to the Poet, pleasures of the imagination. These objects they each respectively pursue, as pleasures adapted to that part of their nature which they have been accustomed to indulge and cultivate.

Now as men will be apt to act consistently with their general views and habitual tendencies, would it not be absurd to expect that the philosopher should look for his sovereign good at a ball, or the sensualist in the pleasures of intellect or piety? None of these ends are answerable to the general views of the respective pursuer; they are not correspondent to his ideas; they are not commensurate to his aims. The sublimest pleasures can afford little gratification where a taste for them has not been previously formed. A clown, who should hear a scholar or an artist talk of the delights of a library, a picture-gallery or a concert, could not guess at the nature of the pleasures they afford; nor would his being introduced to them give him much clearer ideas; because he would bring to them an eye blind to proportion, an understanding new to science, and an ear deaf to harmony.

Shall we expect then, since men can only become scholars by diligent labor, that they shall become Christians by mere chance? Shall we be surprised if those do not fulfil the offices of religion, who are not trained to an acquaintance with them ? And will it not be obvious that it must be some other thing besides the abstruseness of creeds, which has tended to make Christianity unfashionable, and piety obsolete?

It probably will not be disputed, that in no age have the passions of our high-born youth been so early freed from all curb and restraint. In no age has the paternal authority been so contemptuously treated, or every species of subordination so disdainfully trampled upon. In no age have simple, and natural, and youthful pleasures so early lost their power over the mind; nor was ever one great secret of virtue and happiness, the secret of being *cheaply pleased*, so little understood.

A taste for costly, or artificial, or tumultuous pleasures cannot be gratified, even by their most sedulous pursuers, at every moment; and what wretched management is it in the œconomy of human happiness, so to contrive, as that the enjoyment shall be rare and difficult, and the intervals long

and languid! Whereas real and unadulte-
rated pleasures occur perpetually to him
who cultivates a taste for truth and nature,
and science and virtue. But these simple
and tranquil enjoyments cannot but be insipid
to him whose passions have been prema-
turely stimulated by agitating pleasures, or
whose taste has been depraved by such as
are debasing and frivolous; for it is of more
consequence to virtue than some good
people are willing to allow, to preserve the
taste pure, and the judgment sound. A
vitiated intellect has no small connection
with depraved morals.

Since amusements of some kind are
necessary to all ages—I speak now with an
eye to mere human enjoyment—why should
it not be an object of early care, to keep a
due proportion of them in reserve for those
future seasons of life, in which they will be
so much more needed? Why should there
not, even for this purpose, be adopted a
system of salutary restriction, to be used
by parents toward their children, by in-

structors toward their pupils, and in the progress of life by each man toward himself? In a word, why should not the same reasons, which have induced us to tether inferior animals, suggest the expediency of, in some sort, tethering man also? Since nothing but experience seems to teach him, that if he be allowed to anticipate his future possessions, and trample all the flowery fields of real, as well as those of imaginary and artificial enjoyment, he not only endures present disgust, but defaces and destroys all the rich materials of his future happiness; and leaves himself, for the rest of his life, nothing but ravaged fields and barren stubble.

But the great and radical defect, and that which comes more immediately within the present design, seems to be, that in general the characteristical principles of Christianity are not early and strongly infused into the mind: that religion, if taught at all, is rather taught incidentally, as a thing of subordinate value, than as the leading principle of human actions, the great animating spring of human conduct. Were the high influential principles of the Christian religion anxiously and early inculcated, we should find that those lapses from virtue, to which passion and temptation afterwards too frequently solicit, would be more easily recoverable.

For though the evil propensities of fallen nature, and the bewitching allurements of pleasure, will too often seduce even those of the best education into devious paths, yet we shall find that men will seldom be *incurably* wicked unless that internal corruption of principle has taken place, which teaches them how to justify iniquity by argument, and to confirm evil conduct by the sanction of false reasoning ; or where there is a total ignorance of the very nature and design of Christianity, which ignorance can only exist where early religious instruction has been entirely neglected.

The errors occasioned by the violence of passion may be reformed, but systematic

wickedness will be only fortified by time ;
and no decrease of strength, no decay of
appetite, can weaken the power of a pernicious principle.   He who deliberately
commits a bad action, puts himself indeed
out of the path of safety; but he who
adopts a false principle, not only throws
himself into the enemy's country, but burns
the ships, breaks the bridge, cuts off every
retreat by which he might hope one day to
return into his own.

It is remarkable, that in almost all the
celebrated characters of whom we have an
account in former periods of the English
History, we find a serious attention to religion discovering itself at the close of life,
however the preceding years might unhappily have been misemployed.   We meet
with   striking   examples   of   this   kind
amongst statesmen, amongst philosophers,
amongst men of business, and even amongst
men of pleasure.   We have on record the
dying sentiments of *Walsingham*, of *Smith*,
of *Hatton*, the favourites of Queen Eliza-

beth. We see, in the following reign, *Raleigh*, supporting himself by religion under the severity of his fate; *Bacon* seeking comfort in devotion amidst his digraces; and *Wotton*, after having been ambassador to almost every court in Europe, taking refuge at last in a pious retirement at Eton College. But to enumerate instances would be endless, when, in fact, we scarcely discover a single instance to the contrary. In those times, it was considered as a matter even of common decency, that advanced age should possess, at least, the exterior of piety; and we have every reasons to believe that an irreligious old man would have been pointed at as a sort of monster.

But is this the case in our day? Do we now commonly perceive in any rank that disposition to close life religiously, which at the period to which I have alluded was so general even in the fashionable world? I fear it is so far the reverse, that if Pope had been our contemporary, and were now composing his famous Ethical Poem, he could not hazard even that light remark,

That beads and prayer-books are the toys of age,

without grossly violating probability.

But to what cause are we to ascribe that superannuated impiety, which seems to distinguish the present from the preceding generations? Is it not chiefly owing to the neglect of early religious instruction, which now for so many years has been gaining ground among us? In the last age even public schools were places, no less of Christian than of classical institution : and the omission of religious worship, whether public or private, was deemed, at least, as censurable a fault as the neglect of a lesson. Parents had not yet imbibed that maxim of modern refinement, that religious instruction ought to be deferred until the mind be capable of chusing for itself—that is, until it be so pre-occupied as to leave neither room nor relish for the articles of Christian faith, or the rules of Christian

obedience. The advice of the wise king of
Israel of "training up a child in the way
" he should go," had not then become obsolete; and the truth of his assertion, in the
remaining clause of the passage, was hap-
pily realised in the sincere, though late,
return of many a wanderer.

Even in the very laws of our nature,
there seems to be a gracious provision for
promoting the final efficacy of early religious instruction.   When the old man
has no longer any relish left for his accustomed gratifications, in what way does he
endeavour to fill up the void? Is it not by
sending back his thoughts to his early years,
and endeavouring to live over again in idea
those scenes which, in his distant retro-
spect, appear far more delightful than he
had found them to be at the actual period
of enjoyment? Disgusted at every thing
around him, and disappointed in those pursuits to which he had once looked forward
with all the ardour of hope; but to which
he now feels he has sacrificed in vain, his

quiet, and perhaps his integrity, he takes a pensive pleasure in reviewing the season, when his mind was yet cheerful and innocent; and even the very cares and anxieties of that happy period appear to him now, in a more captivating form than any pleasures he can yet hope to enjoy. What then is more natural, I had almost said more certain, than that if the principles of religion were inculcated, and the feelings of devotion excited in his mind in that most susceptible season of life, they should now revive as well as other contemporary impressions, and present themselves in a point of view, the more interesting, because, while all other instances of youthful occupation can be only *recollected*, those may be called up into fresh existence, and be enjoyed even more perfectly than before.

The defects of memory also, which old age induces, will, in this instance, assist rather than obstruct. It almost universally happens, that the more recent transactions are those soonest forgotten, while the events of youth and childhood are remembered with accuracy. If therefore pious principles have been implanted, they will, even by the course of nature, be recollected, while those things which most contributed to hinder their growth, are swept from the memory. What a powerful encouragement then does this consideration afford! or rather what an indispensable obligation does it lay upon parents, to store the minds of their children with the seeds of piety! And on the other hand, what unnatural barbarity is it, irretrievably to shut up this last refuge of the wretched, by a neglect of this duty; and to render it impossible for those who had " stood all the day idle," to be called, at least without a miracle, which the negligent has little right to expect, even at the eleventh hour!

No one surely will impute to bigotry or enthusiasm, the lamenting, or even remonstrating against such desperate negligence;

nor can it be deemed illiberal to inquire,
Whether even a still greater evil does not
exist? I mean, whether pernicious principles
are not as strenuously inculcated as those of
real virtue and happiness are discountenanced? Whether young men are not expressly taught to take custom and fashion
as the ultimate and exclusive standard by
which to try their principles and to weigh
their actions? Whether some idol of false
honour be not consecrated and set up for
them to worship? Whether, even among the
better sort, reputation be not held out as a
motive of sufficient energy to produce virtue, in a world where yet the greatest vices
are every day practised openly, without at
all obstructing the reception, of those who
practise them into the best company?
Whether resentment be not ennobled; and
pride, and many other passions, erected into
honourable virtues—virtues not less repugnant to the genius and spirit of Christianity
than obvious and gross vices? Will it be
thought impertinent to enquire if the awful

doctrines of a perpetually present Deity, a future righteous judgment, and a tremendous responsibility, are early impressed and lastingly engraven on the hearts and consciences of our high-born youth?

Perhaps, if there be any one particular in which we fall remarkably below the politer nations of antiquity, it is in that part of education which has a reference to purity of mind, and the discipline of the heart.

The great secret of religious education, which seems banished from the present practice, consists in training young men to an habitual interior restraint, an early government of the affections, and a course of self-controul over those tyrannizing inclinations which have so natural a tendency to enslave the human heart. Without this habit of moral restraint, which is one of the fundamental laws of Christian virtue, though men may, from natural temper, often *do* good, yet it is impossible that they should ever *be* good. Without the vigorous exercise of this controlling principle, the best dispositions and the most amiable qualities will go but a little way towards establishing a virtuous character. For the best dispositions will be easily overcome by the concurrence of passion within, and temptation without, in a heart where the passions have not been accustomed to this wholesome discipline; and the most amiable qualities will but more easily betray their possessor, unless the heart be fortified by repeated acts and long habits of resistance.

In this, as in various other instances, we may blush at the superiority of Pagan institution. Were the Roman youth taught to imagine themselves always in the awful presence of Cato, in order to habituate them betimes to suppress base sentiments, and to excite such as were generous and noble? And should not the Christian youth be continually reminded, that a greater than Cato is here? Should they not be trained to the habit of acting under the constant impression, that *He* to whom

they must one day be accountable for in-
tentions, as well as words and actions, is
witness to the one as well as the other?
that he not only is " about their path,"
but " understands their very thoughts?"

Were the disciples of a Pagan* leader
taught that it was a motive sufficient to
compel their obedience to any rule, whether
they liked it or not, that it had the authority of their teacher's name? were the bare
words, *the master hath said it*, sufficient to
settle all disputes, and to subdue all reluc-
tance? And shall the scholars of a more
divine teacher, who have a code of laws
written by God himself, be contented with
a lower rule, or abide by a meaner authority? And is any argument drawn from
human considerations likely to operate
more forcibly on a dependant being,
indebted to the Almighty for life, and
breath, and all things, than that simple but
grand assertion, with which so many of

---

* Pythagoras.

the precepts of our religion are introduced—
Because, THUS SAITH THE LORD?

It is doing but little, in the infusion of
first principles, to obtain the bare assent of
the understanding to the existence of one
Supreme Power, unless the heart and affections go along with the conviction, by
our conceiving of that power as intimately
connected with ourselves. A feeling
temper will be but little affected with the
cold idea of a *geometrical* God, as the excellent Pascal expresses it, who merely ad-
justs all the parts of matter, and keeps the
elements in order. Such a mind will be
but little moved, unless he be taught to
consider his Maker under the interesting
and endearing representation which revealed religion gives of him. That " God
" is," will be to him rather an alarming
than a consolatory idea; till he be persuaded
of the subsequent proposition, that " he is
" a Rewarder of them that diligently seek
" him." Nay, if natural religion *does*
even acknowledge one awful attribute,

that " God is just," it will only increase
the terror of a tender conscience, till it be
learned from the fountain of truth, that he
is " the Justifier of him who believeth in
" Jesus."

But if the great sanctions of our religion
are not deeply engraven on the heart,
where shall we look for any other adequate
curb to the fiery spirit of youth? For, let
the elements be ever so kindly mixed in a
human composition, let the natural temper
be ever so amiable, still whenever a man
ceases to think himself an accountable
being, what motive can he have for resisting
a strong temptation to a present good,
when he has no dread that he shall thereby
forfeit a greater future good?

It may perhaps be objected, that this
deep sense of religion would interfere with
the general purpose of education, which is
designed to qualify men for the business of
human life, and not to train up a race of
monks and ascetics.

There is however so little real solidity in

this specious objection, that I am firmly persuaded, that if religious principles were more deeply impressed on the heart, even the things of this world would be much better carried on. For where are we to look for all the qualities which constitute the man of business; for punctuality, diligence, and application, for such attention in doing every thing in its proper day, (the great hinge on which business turns,) as among men of principle? Oeconomy of time, truth in observing his word, never daring to deceive or to disappoint—these form the very essence of an active and an useful character; and for these to whom shall we most naturally look? Who is so little likely to be " slothful in business" as he who is " fervent in spirit?" And will not he be most regular in dealing with men, who is most diligent in " serving the " Lord?"

But, it may be said, allowing that religion does not necessarily spoil a man of *business*, yet it would effectually defeat

those accomplishments, and counteract that
fine breeding, which essentially constitute
the *gentleman.*

This again is so far from being a natural
consequence, that, supposing all the other
real advantages of parts, education, and
society, to be equally taken into the account, there is no doubt but that, in point
of true politeness, a real Christian would
beat the world at its own weapons, the
world itself being judge.

It must be confessed that, in the present
corrupt state of things, there is scarcely
any one contrivance for which we are more
obliged to the inventions of mankind than
for that of politeness, as there is perhaps
no screen in the world which hides so many
ugly sights. Yet while we allow that there
never was so admirable a substitute for real
goodness as good breeding, it is certain
that the principles of Christianity put into
action, would of themselves produce more
genuine politeness than any maxims drawn
from motives of human vanity, desire of ad-

miration, or worldly convenience. If *love,
peace, joy, long suffering, gentleness, patience,
goodness, and meekness,* may be thought in-
struments to produce sweetness of manners,
these we are expressly told are " the fruits
of the " spirit." If mourning with the af-
flicted, rejoicing with the happy; if to " es-
" teem others better than ourselves;" if " to
" take the lowest room ;" if " not to seek
" our own ;" if " not to behave ourselves
" unseemly; if " not to speak great swel-
" ling words of vanity"—if these are
amiable, engaging, and polite parts of
behaviour, then would the documents of
Saint Paul make as true a fine gentleman
as the *Courtier of Castiglione,* or even the
Letters of Lord Chesterfield himself. Then
would simulation, and dissimulation, and
all the nice shades and delicate gradations
of passive and active deceit, be rendered
superfluous; and the affections of every
heart be won by a shorter and a surer way
than by the elegant obliquities of this late
popular preceptor, whose mischiefs have

M

outlived his reputation; and who, notwithstanding the present just declension of
his fame, greatly contributed, during its
transient meridian, to relax the general
nerve of virtue, and who has left a taint
upon the public morals, of which we are
still sensible.

That self-abasement then, which is inseparable from true Christianity, the external signs of which good-breeding knows
so well how to assume; and those charities which suggest invariable kindness
to others, even in the smallest things,
would, if left to their natural workings,
produce that gentleness which it is one
great object of a polite education to imitate.
They would produce it too without effort
and without exertion; for being inherent
in the substance, it would naturally discover itself on the surface.

For however useful the institutions of
polished society may be found, yet they
can never alter the eternal difference
between right and wrong, or convert appear-

ances into realities ; they cannot transform
decency into virtue, nor make politeness
pass for principle. And the advocates for
fashionable breeding should be humbled to
reflect, that every convention of artificial
manners was adopted not to *cure*, but to
conceal, deformity : that though the
superficial civilities of elegant life tend to
make this corrupt world a more tolerable
place than it would be without them, yet
they never will be considered as a substitute for truth, nor a commutation for
virtue, by HIM who is to pass the defini-
tive sentence on the characters of men.

Among the many prejudices which the
young and the gay entertain against religion, one is, that it is the declared enemy
to wit and genius. But, says one of its
wittiest champions,* " Piety enjoins no
" man to be dull :" and it will be found,
on a fair enquiry, that though it cannot be
denied that irreligion has had able men for

* Dr. South.

M 2

its advocates, yet they have never been the *most* able. Nor can any learned profession, any department in letters or in science, produce a champion on the side of unbelief, but Christianity has a still greater name to oppose to it ; *philosophers* themselves being judges.

Newton, who studied the book of nature with a scrutiny which has never been permitted to any other mortal eye, was deeply learned in the book of God. And the ablest writer on the intellect of man, has left one of the ablest treatises *on the Reasonableness of Christianity.* The essay of Mr. Locke on the *Human Understanding* will stand up to latest ages, as a monument of wisdom ; while Hume's posthumous work, *the Essay on Suicide,* which had excited such large expectations, has been long since forgotten.*

---

* The Essay on Suicide was published soon after Mr. Hume's death. It might mortify his liberal mind (if matter and motion were capable of conscious-

. Pascal has proved that as much rhetoric
and logic too may be shown in defending
revelation as in attacking it.   His geometrical spirit was not likely to take up with

ness) to learn, that this his dying legacy, the last
concentrated effort of his genius and his principles,
sent from the grave, as it were, by a man so justly
renowned in other branches of literature, produced no
sensation on the public mind.   And that the precious
information that every man had a right to be his own
executioner, was considered as a privilege so little desi-
rable, that it probably had not the glory of converting
one *cross road* into a cemetery.   It is to the credit of
this country that fewer copies of this work were sold
than perhaps ever was the case with a writer of so
much eminence.   A more impotent act of wickedness
has seldom been achieved, or one which has had the
glory of making fewer persons wicked or miserable.
That cold and cheerless oblivion which he held out
as a refuge to beings who had solaced themselves with
the soothing hope of immortality has, by a memorable
retribution, overshadowed his own last labour: the
Essay on Suicide being already as much forgotten
as he promised the best men that they themselves would
be.   And this favourite work became at once a
prey to that eternal night to which he had consigned the
whole human race.

any proofs but such as came as near to demonstration as the nature of the subject
would admit. *Erasmus* in his writings on
the ignorance of the Monks, and the Pro-
vincial Letters on the fallacies of the
Jesuits, while they exhibit as entire a
freedom from bigotry, exhibit also as much
pointed wit, and as much sound reasoning,
as can be found in the whole mass of
modern Philosophy.

But while the young adopt the opinion
from one class of writers, that religious
men are weak men, they acquire from
another class a notion that they are ridiculous. And this opinion, by mixing itself
with their common notions, and deriving
itself from their very amusements, is the
more mischievous, as it is imbibed without
suspicion, and entertained without resistance.

One common medium through which
they take this false view is, those favourite
works of wit and humour, so captivating
to youthful imaginations, where no small

part of the author's success perhaps, has
been owing to his dexterously introducing
a pious character with so many virtues,
that it is impossible not to love him ; yet
tinctured with so many absurdities, that it
is equally impossible not to laugh at him.
The reader's memory will furnish him with
too many instances of what is here meant.
The slightest touches of a witty malice can
make the best character ridiculous. It is
effected by any little awkwardness, absence
of mind, an obsolete phrase, a formal pro-
nunciation, a peculiarity of gesture. Or
if such a character be brought by unsus-
pecting honesty, and credulous goodness
into some foolish scrape, it will stamp on
him an impression of ridicule so indelible,
that all his worth shall not be able to efface
it : and the young, who do not always separate their ideas very carefully, shall ever
after, by this early and false association,
conceive of piety as having something essentially ridiculous in itself.

But one of the most infallible arts by

which the inexperienced are engaged on the side of irreligion, is that popular air of candour, good-nature, and toleration, which it so invariably puts on. While sincere piety is often accused of moroseness and severity, because it cannot hear the doctrines on which it founds its eternal hopes derided without emotion; indifference and unbelief purchase the praise of candour at an easy price, because they neither suffer grief nor express indignation at hearing the most awful truths ridiculed, or the most solemn obligations set at nought. The two parties do not engage on equal terms. The infidel appears good humoured from his very levity; but the Christian cannot jest on subjects which involve his everlasting salvation.

The prophane wits whom young people hear talk, and the books which they hear quoted, falsely charge their own injurious opinions on Christianity, and then unjustly accuse her of being the monster they have made. They dress her up with the sword of

persecution in one hand, and the flames
of intolerance in the other; and then
ridicule the sober-minded for worshipping
an idol which their misrepresentation has
rendered as malignant as Moloch. In the
mean time they affect to seize on benevolence with exclusive appropriation as their
own cardinal virtue, and to accuse of a
bigotted cruelty, that narrow spirit which
points out the perils of licentiousness, and
the terrors of a future account. And yet
this benevolence, with all its tender mer-
cies, is not afraid nor ashamed to endeavour at snatching away from humble piety
the comfort of a present hope, and the
bright prospect of a felicity that shall have
no end. It does not, however, seem a very
probable means of increasing the stock of
human happiness, to plunder mankind of
that principle, by the destruction of which
friendship is robbed of its bond, society of
its security, patience of its motive, morality
of its foundation, integrity of its reward,

sorrow of its consolation, life of its balm, and death of its support.*

It will not perhaps be one of the meanest advantages of a better state that, as the will shall be reformed, so the judgment shall be rectified; that " evil shall no more " be called good," nor the " churl liberal;" nor the plunderer of our best possession, our principles, *benevolent*. Then it will be evident that greater injury could not be done to truth, nor greater violence to language, than by attempting to wrest from Christianity that benevolence which is in

* Young persons too are liable to be misled by that extreme disingenuousness of the new philosophers, when writing on every thing and person connected with revealed religion. These authors often quote satirical poets as grave historical authorities; for instance, because Juvenal has said that the Jews were so narrow-minded that they refused to show a spring of water, or the right road to an inquiring traveller who was not of their religion, I make little doubt but many an ignorant free-thinker has actually gone away with the belief, that such good-natured acts of information were actually forbidden by the law of Moses.

fact her most appropriate and peculiar attribute. —" A new commandment give I
" unto you, that ye love one another."
If benevolence be " good will to men," it
was that which angelic messengers were not
thought too high to announce, nor a much
higher being than Angels too great to teach
by his example, and to illustrate by his
death. It was the criterion, the very
watch word, as it were, by which he intended his religion and his followers should
be distinguished. " By this shall all men
" know that ye are my disciples, if ye
" have love one to another." Besides, it
is the very genius of Christianity to extir-
pate selfishness, that tenacious and last sur-
viving corruption, on whose vacated ground
benevolence naturally and necessarily plants
itself.

But not to run through all the particu-
lars which obstruct the growth of piety in
young persons, I shall only name one more.
They hear much declamation from the
fashionable reasoners against the contracted

and interested spirit of Christianity—that it is of a sordid temper, works for pay, and looks for reward.

This jargon of French philosophy, which prates of pure disinterested goodness acting for its own sake, and equally despising punishment and disdaining recompense, indicates as little knowledge of human nature as of Christian revelation, when it addresses man as a being made up of pure intellect, without any mixture of passions, and who can be made happy without hope, and virtuous without fear. These Philosophers affect to be more independent than Moses, more disinterested than Christ himself; for "Moses had respect to the recompence of "reward;" and Christ "endured the cross "and despised the shame, for the joy that "was set before him."

A creature hurried away by the impulse of some impetuous inclination, is not likely to be restrained, if he be restrained at all, by a cold reflection on the beauty of virtue. If the dread of offending God, and incurring his everlasting displeasure, cannot stop his career, how shall a weaker motive do it? When we see that the powerful sanctions which religion holds out are too often an ineffectual curb; to think of attaining the same end by feebler means, is as if one should expect to make a watch go the better by breaking the main-spring; nay, as absurd as if the philosopher who inculcates the doctrine should undertake, with one of his fingers, to lift an immense weight which had resisted the powers of the crane and the lever.

On calm and temperate spirits indeed, in the hour of retirement, in the repose of the passions, in the absence of temptation, virtue does seem to be her own adequate reward; and very lovely are the fruits she bears in preserving health, credit, and fortune. But on how few will this principle act! and even on them how often will its operation be suspended! And though virtue for her own sake might have captivated a few hearts, which should almost seem cast in a natural mould of goodness, if such mould there were, yet no motive could, at all times, be so likely to restrain even these, especially under the pressure of temptation, as this simple assertion—*For all this, God will bring thee into judgment.*

It is the beauty of our religion, that it is not held out exclusively to a few select spirits; that it is not an object of speculation, or an exercise of ingenuity, but a scheme of Salvation, but a *rule of life,* suited to every condition, capacity, and temper. It is the glory of the Christian religion to *be,* what it was the glory of every antient philosophic system *not* to be, *the religion of the people;* and that which constitutes its characteristic value, is its suitableness to the genius, condition, and necessities of all mankind.

For with whatsoever obscurities it has pleased God to shadow some parts of his written word, yet he has graciously ordered, that whatever is necessary should be perspicuous also: and though, as to his adorable essence, " clouds and darkness are round

" about him;" yet these are not the medium
through which he has left us to discover
our duty. In this, as in all other points,
revealed religion has a decided superiority
over all the antient systems of philosophy,
which were always in many respects impracticable and extravagant, because not framed
from observations drawn from a perfect
knowledge " of what was in man." Whereas
the whole scheme of the Gospel is accommodated to real human nature ; laying open
its mortal disease, presenting its only remedy;
exhibiting rules of conduct, often difficult,
indeed, but never impossible; and where
the rule was so high that the practicability
seemed desperate, holding out in its great
author, a living pattern, to elucidate the
doctrine and to illustrate the precept;
offering every where the clearest notions of
what we have to hope, and what we have to
fear ; the strongest injunctions of what we
are to believe, and the most explicit direc-
tions of what we are to do. And crowning
all with the most encouraging offers of Di-

vine assistance for strengthening our faith and quickening our obedience.

In short, whoever examines the wants of his own heart, and the appropriate assistance which the Gospel furnishes, will find them to be two tallies which exactly correspond—an internal evidence, stronger perhaps than any other, of the truth of revelation.

This is the religion with which the ingenuous hearts of youth should be warmed, and by which their minds, while pliant, should be directed. This will afford a "lamp to their paths," stronger, steadier, brighter, than the feeble and uncertain glimmer of a cold and comfortless philosophy.

CHAPTER IV.

*Other Symptoms of the Decline of Christianity
—No Family Religion—Corrupt or negligent Example of Superiors—The Self-denying and Evangelical Virtues held in contempt—Neglect of encouraging and promoting Religion among Servants.*

IT was by no means the design of the present undertaking to make a general invective on the corrupt state of manners, or
even to animadvert on the conduct of the
higher ranks, but inasmuch as the corruption of that conduct, and the depravation
of those manners, appear to be a natural
consequence of the visible decline of religion; and as operating in its turn, as a
cause, on the inferior orders of society.

Of the other obvious causes which contribute to this decline of morals, little will
be said. Nor is the present a romantic at-

tempt to restore the simplicity of primitive
manners. This is too literally an age of
gold, to expect that it should be so in the
poetical and figurative sense. It would be
unjust and absurd nor to form our opinions
and expectations from the present general
state of society. And it would argue great
ignorance of the corruption which commerce, and conquest, and riches, and arts,
necessarily introduce into a state, to look
for the same sobermindedness, simplicity,
and purity among the *dregs of Romulus,*
as the severe and simple manners of elder
Rome presented.

But though it would be an attempt of
desperate hardihood, to controvert that
maxim of the witty bard, that

To mend the world's a vast design;

a popular aphorism, by the way, which has
done no little mischief, inasmuch, as under
the mask of hopelessness it suggests an indolent acquiescence; yet to make the best
of the times in which we live; to fill up the

measure of our own actual, particular, and individual duties; and to take care that the age shall not be the worse for our having been cast into it, seems to be the bare dictate of common probity, and not a romantic flight of impracticable perfection.

Is it then so very chimerical to imagine, that the benevolent can be sober-minded? Is it romantic to desire, that the virtuous should be consistent? Is it absurd to fancy that what has once been practised should not now be impracticable?

It is impossible not to help regretting, that it should be the general temper of many of the leading persons of that age, which arrogates to itself the glorious character of the *age of benevolence*, to be kind, considerate, and compassionate, every where rather than at home; that the rich and the fashionable should be zealous in promoting religious as well as charitable institutions abroad, and yet discourage every thing which looks like religion in their own families: that they should be at a consider-

able expence in instructing the poor at a
distance, and yet discredit piety among
their own servants—those more immediate
objects of every man's attention, whom
Providence has enabled to keep any; and
for whose conduct he will be finally accountable, inasmuch as he may have helped, by
his practice or his negligence, to corrupt it.

Is there any degree of pecuniary bounty
without doors which can counteract the
mischief of a wrong conduct at home, or
atone for that infectious laxity of principle
which spreads corruption wherever its influence extends? Is not he the best benefactor to society who sets the best example,
and who does not only the most good, but
the least evil? Will not that man, however
liberal, very imperfectly promote virtue in
the world at large, who neglects to disse-
minate its principles within the immediate
sphere of his own personal influence, by a
correct conduct and a blameless behaviour?
Can a generous, but profligate, person atone
by his purse for the disorders of his life?

Can he expect a blessing on his bounties, while he defeats their effect by a profane or even a careless conversation?

In moral as well as in political treatises, it is often asserted, that it is a great evil to do no good, but it has not been, perhaps, enough insisted on, that it is a great good to do no evil. This species of goodness is not ostentatious enough for popular declamation; and the value of this abstinence from vice is, perhaps, not well understood but by Christians, because it wants the ostensible brilliancy of actual performance.

But as the *principles* of Christianity are in no great repute, so their concomitant *qualities*, the evangelical virtues, are proportionably disesteemed. Let it, however, be remembered, that those secret habits of self-controul, those interior and unobtrusive virtues, which excite no astonishment, kindle no emulation, and extort no praise, are, at the same time, the most difficult, and the most sublime; and if Christianity be true, will be the most graciously accepted by *him* who witnesses the secret combat and the silent victory : while the splendid deeds which have the world for their witness, and immortal fame for their reward, shall, perhaps, cost him who achieved them less than it costs a conscientious Christian to subdue one irregular inclination; a conquest which the world will never know; and, if it did, would probably despise.

Though great actions performed on human motives, are permitted by the supreme Disposer to be equally beneficial to society with such as are performed on purer principles; yet it is an affecting consideration, that, at the final adjustment of accounts, the politician who *raised* a state, or the hero who *preserved* it, may miss of that favour of God which, if it was not his motive, will certainly not be his reward. And it is awful to reflect, as we visit the monuments justly raised by public gratitude, or the statues properly erected by well-earned admiration; it is awful, I say, to reflect on what may now be the unalterable condition

of the illustrious object of these deserved
but unavailing honours; it is awful to
reflect that he who has saved a state may
have lost his own soul!

A Christian life seems to consist of two
things, almost equally difficult; the adoption of good habits, and the excision of
such as are evil. No one sets out on a
religious course with a stock of native innocence, or actual freedom from sin; for
there is no such state in human life. The
natural heart is not, as has been too often
supposed, a blank paper, whereon the divine
spirit has nothing to do but to stamp characters of goodness: no! many blots are
to be erased, many defilements are to be
cleansed, as well as fresh impressions to be
made.

The vigilant Christian, therefore, who
acts with an eye to the approbation of his
Maker, rather than to that of mankind,
to a future account, rather than to present
glory, will find that, diligently to cultivate
the "unweeded garden" of his own heart;

to mend the soil; to clear the ground of its indigenous vices, by practising the painful business of extirpation, will be that part of his duty which will cost him most labour, and bring him least credit: while the fair flower of one shewy action, produced with little trouble, and of which the very pleasure is reward enough, shall gain him more praise than the eradication of the rankest weeds which over-run the natural heart.

But the Gospel judges not after the manner of men; for it never fails to make the abstinent virtues a previous step to the right performance of the operative ones; and the relinquishing what is wrong to be a necessary prelude to the performance of what is right. It makes " ceasing to " do evil" the indispensable preliminary to " learning to do well." It continually suggests that something is to be laid aside, as well as to be practised. We must " hate vain thoughts," before we can " love God's law." We must lay aside " malice and hypocrisy," to *enable* us

" to receive the engrafted word.—Having " a conscience void of offence;"
" abstaining from fleshly lusts;" bring-
" ing every thought into obedience;"—
these are actions, or rather negations,
which though they never will obtain immortality from the chisel of the statuary,
the declamation of the historian, or the
panegyric of the poet, will, however, be
"had in everlasting remembrance," when
the works of the statuary, the historian,
and the poet will be no more.

   And, for our encouragement, is it obser-
vable that a more difficult Christian virtue
generally involves an easier one. A
habit of self-denial in permitted pleasures,
easily induces a victory over such as are
unlawful. And to sit loose to our own
possessions, necessarily includes an exemption from coveting the possessions of
others: and so on of the rest.

   Will it be difficult then to trace back to
that want of early restraint noticed in the
preceding chapter, that licence of behaviour

which, having been indulged in youth, afterwards reigns uncontrolled in families; and which having infected education in its first springs, taints all the streams of domestic virtue? And will it be thought strange that that same want of religious principle which corrupted our children, should corrupt our servants?

We scarcely go into any company without hearing some invective against the increased profligacy of this order of men; and the remark is made with as great an air of astonishment, as if the cause of the complaint were not as visible as the truth of it. It would be endless to point out instances in which the increased dissipation of their *betters* (as they are oddly called) has contributed to the growth of this evil. But it comes only within the immediate design of the present undertaking, to insist on the single circumstance of the almost total extermination of religion in fashionable families, as a cause adequate of itself to any consequence which depraved morals can produce.

Is there not a degree of injustice in persons who express strong indignation at those crimes which crowd our prisons, and furnish our incessant executions, and who yet discourage not an internal principle of vice: since those crimes are nothing more than that principle put into action? And it is no less absurd than cruel, in such of the great as lead disorderly lives, to expect to prevent vice by the laws they make to restrain or punish it, while their own example is a perpetual source of temptation to commit it. If, by their own practice, they demonstrate that they think a vicious or a careless life is the only happy one, with what colour of justice can they inflict penalties on others, who, by acting on the same principle, naturally expect the same indulgence!

And indeed it is somewhat unreasonable to expect very high degrees of virtue and probity from a class of people whose whole life, after they are admitted into dissipated families, is one continued counteraction of

the principles in which they have probably
been bred.

When a poor youth is transplanted from
one of those excellent institutions which do
honour to the present age, and give some
hope of reforming the next, into the family
of his noble benefactor in town, who has,
perhaps, provided liberally for his instruction in the country; what must be his
astonishment at finding the manner of life
to which he is introduced diametrically opposite to that life to which he has been
taught that salvation is alone annexed! He
has been taught that it was his bounden
duty to be devoutly thankful for his own
scanty meal, perhaps of barley-bread ; yet
he sees his noble lord sit down every day

Not to a dinner, but a hecatomb ;

to a repast for which every element is plundered, and every climate impoverished; for
which nature is ransacked, and art is exhausted; without even the formal ceremony

of a slight acknowledgment. It will be fortunate for the master, if his servant does not happen to know that even the Pagans never sat down to a repast without making a libation to their deities; and that the Jews did not eat a little fruit, or drink a cup of water, without an expression of devout thankfulness.

Next to the law of God, he has been taught to reverence the law of the land, and to respect an act of parliament next to a text of Scripture: yet he sees his honourable protector publicly in his own house, engaged in the evening in playing at a game expressly prohibited by the laws, and against which perhaps he himself had been assisting in the day to pass an act.

While the contempt of religion was confined to wits and philosophers, the effect was not so sensibly felt. But we cannot congratulate the ordinary race of mortals on their emancipation from the old prejudices, or their indifference to usages, which long prescription has rendered sacred

in their eyes; as it is not at all visible that
the world is become happier in proportion as
it is become more enlightened. We might
rejoice more in the boasted diffusion of
light and freedom, were it not apparent
that bankruptcies are grown more frequent,
robberies more common, divorces more
numerous, and forgeries more extensive—
that more rich men die by their own hand,
and more poor men by the hand of the
executioner—than when Christianity was
practised by the vulgar, and countenanced,
at least, by the great.

It is not to be regretted, therefore, while
the affluent are encouraging so many admirable schemes for promoting religion among
the children of the poor, that they do not
like to *perpetuate* the principle, by encouraging it in their own children and their
servants also? Is it not pity, since these last
are so moderately furnished with the good
things of this life, to rob them of that
bright reversion, the bare hope of which
is a counterpoise to all the hardships they

undergo here—especially since by diminishing this future hope, we shall not be likely
to add to their present usefulness?

Still allowing, what has been already
granted, that absolute infidelity is not the
reigning evil, and that servants will perhaps
be more likely to see religion neglected,
than to hear it ridiculed,—would it not be
a meritorious kindness in families of a better
stamp, to furnish them with more opportunities of learning and practising their
duty? Is it not impolitic indeed, as well
as unkind, to refuse them any means of
having impressed on their consciences the
operative principles of Christianity? It is
but little, barely not to *oppose* their going
to church, not to *prevent* their doing their
duty at home; their opportunities of doing
both ought to be facilitated, by giving them,
at certain seasons, as few employments as
possible that may interfere with both. Even
when religion is by pretty general consent
banished from our families at home, that
only furnishes a stronger reason why our

families should not be banished from religion in the churches.

But if these opportunities are not made easy and convenient to them, their superiors have no right to expect from them a zeal so far transcending their own, as to induce them to surmount difficulties for the sake of duty. Religion is never once represented in scripture as a light attainment; it is never once illustrated by an easy, a quiet, or an indolent allegory. On the contrary, it is exhibited under the active figure of a combat, a race; something expressive of exertion, activity, progress. And yet many are unjust enough to think that this warfare can be fought, though they themselves are perpetually weakening the vigour of the combatant; this race be run, though they are incessantly obstructing the progress of him who runs by some hard and interfering command. That our compassionate Judge, who " knoweth whereof we are " made, and remembereth that we are but " dust," is particularly touched with the feeling of *their* infirmities, can never be doubted; but what portion of forgiveness he will extend to those who lay on their virtue hard burdens "too heavy for them " to bear," who shall say?

To keep an immortal being in a state of spiritual darkness, is a positive disobedience to *His* law, who when he bestowed the Bible, no less than when he created the material world, said, *Let there be light.* It were well, both for the advantage of master and servant, that the latter should have the doctrines of the Gospel frequently impressed on his heart; that his conscience should be made familiar with a system which offers such clear and intelligible propositions of moral duty. The striking interrogation, "how shall I do this great " wickedness, and sin against God?" will perhaps operate as forcibly on an unculti- vated mind, as the most eloquent essay to prove that man is not an accountable being. That once credited promise, that "they " who have done well shall go into ever-

" lasting life," will be more grateful to
the spirit of a plain man, than that more
elegant and disinterested sentiment, that
virtue is its own reward. That " he that
" walketh uprightly walketh surely," is
not on the whole a dangerous, or a mis-
leading maxim. And " well done, good
" and faithful servant! I will make thee
" ruler over many things," though a promise offensive to the liberal spirit of philosophic dignity, is a comfortable support to
humble and oppressed, and suffering piety.
That " we should do to others as we
" would they should do to us," is a portable measure of human duty, always at
hand, as always referring to something
within himself, not amiss for a poor man to
carry constantly about with him, who has
neither time nor learning to search for a
better. It is an universal and compendious
law, so universal as to include the whole
compass of social obligation; so compendious as to be inclosed in so short and plain
an aphorism; that the dullest mind cannot misapprehend, nor the weakest

memory forget it. It is convenient for bringing out on all the ordinary occasions of life, and for practising in every possibility of human intercourse. "We need not say "who shall go up to heaven and bring "it unto us, for this word is very nigh "unto thee, in thy mouth and in thy heart, "that thou mayest do it."*

. For it is a very valuable part of the gospel of Christ, that though it is an entire and perfect system in its design ; though it exhibits one great plan, from which complete trains of argument, and connected schemes of reasoning may be deduced; yet in compassion to the multitude, for whom this benevolent institution was in a good measure designed, and who could not have comprehended a long chain of propositions, or have embraced remote deductions, the most important truths of doctrine, and the most essential documents of virtue, are detailed in single maxims, and comprised in short sentences; inde-

* Deut. xxx. 11 and 12.

pendent of themselves, yet making a necessary part of a consummate whole; from a
few of which principles the whole train of
human virtues has been deduced, and many
a perfect body of ethics has been framed.

If it be thought wonderful, that from so
few letters of the alphabet, so few figures of
arithmetic, so few notes in music, such
endless combinations should have been produced in their respective arts; how far
more beautiful would it be to trace the
whole circle of practical virtues thus
growing out of a few elementary principles of gospel truth.

All Seneca's arguments against the fear
of death, though powerful as human wisdom, and unassisted reason could suggest,
never yet reconciled one reader to its
approach, half so effectually as the humble
believer is reconciled to it by that simple
persuasion, " I know that my Redeemer
" liveth."

While the modern philosopher is extending the boundaries of human know-

ledge, by undertaking to prove that matter is eternal; or enlarging the stock of human happiness, by demonstrating the extinction of spirit,—it can do no harm to an unlettered man to believe, that " heaven and " earth shall pass away, but God's word " shall not pass away." While the former is indulging the profitable enquiry why the Deity made the world so late, or why he made it at all, it will not hurt the latter to believe, that " in the beginning God made " the world," and that in the end " he " shall judge it in righteousness."

While the liberal scholar is usefully studying the law of nature and of nations, let him rejoice that his more illiterate brother possesses the plain conviction that " love " is the fulfilling of the law"—that " love " working no ill to his neighbour." And let him be persuaded that he himself, though he know all Tully's offices by heart, may not have acquired a more feeling and operative sentiment than is conveyed to the *common* Christian in the rule to " bear each other's

" burthens." While the wit is criticising the
creed, he will be no loser by encouraging his
dependents to keep the commandments; since
a few such simple propositions as the above
furnish a more practical and correct rule of life
than can be gleaned from all the volumes
of ancient philosophy, justly eminent as
many of them are for wisdom and purity.
For though they abound with passages of
true sublimity, and sentiments of great
moral beauty, yet the result is naturally
defective, the conclusions necessarily contra-
dictory. This was no fault of the author,
but of the system. The vision was acute,
but the light was dim. The sharpest
sagacity could not distinguish spiritual
objects, in the twilight of natural religion,
with that accuracy with which they are now
discerned by every common Christian, in
the diffusion of gospel light.

And whether it be that what depraves
the principle darkens the intellect also, certain it is that an uneducated serious Christian
reads his bible with a clearness of intelli-

gence, with an intellectual perception, which no sceptic or mere worldling ever attains. The plain Christian has not pre-judged the cause he is examining. He is not often led by his passions, still more rarely by his interest, to resist his convictions. While " the secret of the Lord is " (obviously) with them that fear him," the mind of them who fear him *not*, is generally prejudiced by a retaining fee from the world, from their passions or their pride, before they enter on the enquiry. The decision is made before the inquiry is begun.

With what consistency can the covetous man embrace a religion which so pointedly forbids him to lay up "treasures upon earth?" How will the man of spirit, as the world is pleased to call the duellist, relish a religion which allows not " the sun to go down " upon his wrath?" How can the ambitious struggle for " a kingdom which is " not of this world," and embrace a faith which commands him to lay down his

crown at the feet of another? How should
the professed wit or the mere philosopher
adopt a system which demands in a lofty
tone of derision, "Where is the scribe?
"Where is the wife? Where is the disputer
"of this world?" How will the self-satisfied
formalist endure a religion which, while it
peremptorily demands from him every useful action, and every right exertion, will
not permit him to rest his hope of salvation
on their performance? He whose affections
are voluntarily rivetted to the present world,
will not much delight in a scheme whose
avowed principle is to set him above it.—
The obvious consequence of these "hard
"sayings" is illustrated by daily instances.—
"Have any of the rulers believed on him?"
is a question not confined to the first age
of his appearance. Had the most enlightened philosophers of the most polished
nations, collected all the scattered wit and
learning of the world into one point in order
to invent a religion for the salvation of mankind, the doctrine of the cross is perhaps

precisely the thing they would never have
hit upon; precisely the thing which, being
offered to them, they would reject. The
intellectual pride of the philosopher relished
it as little as the worldly pride of the Jew;
for it flattered human wit no more than it
gratified human grandeur. The self-sufficiency of great acquirements, and of great
wealth, equally obstructs the reception of
divine truth into the heart; and whether
the natural man be called upon to part
either from " great possessions," or " high
" imaginations," he equally goes away sor-
rowing.

CHAPTER V.

The negligent Conduct of Christians no real Objection against Christianity.—The reason why its Effects are not more manifest to Worldly Men, is, because Believers do not lead Christian Lives.—Professors differ but little in their Practice from Unbelievers.—Even real Christians are too diffident and timid, and afraid of acting up to their Principles.—The Absurdity of the Charge commonly brought against religious People, that they are too strict.

It is an objection frequently brought against Christianity, that if it exhibited so perfect a scheme, if its influences were as strong, if its effects were as powerful, as its friends pretend, it must have produced more visible consequences in the reformation of mankind. This is not the place fully to answer this objection, which, like all the other cavils against our religion, continues to be urged just as importunately as if it never *had* been answered.

That vice and immorality prevail in no small degree in countries professing Christianity, we need not go out of our own to be convinced. But that this is the case only because this benign principle is not suffered to operate in its full power, will be no less obvious to all who are sincere in their enquiries: For if we allow (and who that examines impartially can help allowing?) that it is the natural tendency of Christianity to make men better, then it must be the aversion from receiving it as a practical principle, and not the fault of the principle itself, which prevents them from becoming so.

Those who are acquainted with the effects which Christianity actually produced in the first ages of the church, when it *was* received in its genuine purity, and when it *did* operate without obstruction, from its

professors at least, will want no other proof
of its inherent power and efficacy. At that
period, its most decided and industrious
enemy, the emperor Julian, could recommend the *manners* of the Galileans to the
imitation of his Pagan high priest; though
he himself, at the same time, was doing
every thing which the most inveterate malice, sharpened by the acutest wit, and
backed by the most absolute power, could
devise, to discredit their doctrines.

Nor would the efficacy of Christianity be
less visible now in influencing the conduct
of its professors, if its doctrines were
heartily and sincerely received. They
would, were they of the true genuine cast
of the Gospel, operate on the conduct so
effectually, that we should see morals and
manners growing out of principles, as we
see other consequences grow out of their
proper and natural causes. Let but this great
spring have its unobstructed play, and there
would be little occasion to declaim against
this excess or that enormity. If the same

skill and care which are employed in curing
symptoms, were vigorously levelled at the
internal principle of the disease, the moral
health would feel the benefit. If that
attention which is bestowed in lopping the
redundant and unsightly branches, were
devoted to the cultivation of a sound and
uncorrupt root, the effect of this labour
would soon be discovered by the excellence
of the fruits.

For though, even in the highest possible
exertion of religious principle, and the most
diligent practices of all its consequential train
of virtues, man would still find evil propensities enough, in his fallen nature, to make
it necessary that he should counteract them,
by keeping alive his diligence after higher
attainments, and to quicken his aspirations
after a better state; yet the prevailing temper would be in general right, the will
would be in a great measure rectified; and
the heart, feeling and acknowledging its
disease, would apply itself diligently to the
only remedy. Thus though even the best

men have infirmities enough to deplore, though they commit sins enough to keep them deeply humble, and feel more sensibly than others the corruption of their nature, and the imperfections of that vessel in which their heavenly treasure is hid, they however have the internal consolation of knowing that they shall have to do with a merciful Father, who "despiseth not the "sighing of the contrite heart, nor the "desire of such as be sorrowful;" with a gracious judge who has been witness to all their struggles against sin, and to whom they can appeal with Peter for the sincerity of their desires—"Lord! Thou knowest "all things. Thou knowest that I love Thee."

All the heavy charges which have been brought against religion, have been taken from the abuses of it. In every other instance, the injustice of this proceeding would be notorious: but there is a general want of candour in the judgment of men on this subject, which we do not find them

exercise on other occasions; that of throwing the fault of the erring or ignorant professor on the profession itself.

It does not derogate from the honourable
profession of arms, that there are cowards
and braggarts in the army. If any man
lose his estate by the chicanery of an attor-
ney, or his health by the blunder of a physician, it is commonly said that the one was
a disgrace to his business, and the other
was ignorant of it; but no one therefore
concludes as a natural inference, that law
and physic are contemptible professions.

Christianity alone is obliged to bear all
the obloquy incurred by the misconduct of
its followers; to sustain all the reproach
excited by ignorant, by fanatical, by superstitious, or hypocritical professors. But
whoever accuses it of a tendency to produce the errors of these professors, must
have picked up his opinion any where
rather than in the New Testament; which
Book being the only authentic history of
Christianity, is that which candour would
naturally consult for information.

But as worldly and irreligious men do
not draw their notions from that pure fountain, but from the polluted stream of human
practice; as they form their judgment of
divine truth from the conduct of those who
pretend to be enlightened by it; some charitable allowance *must* be made for the contempt which they entertain for Christianity,
when they see what poor effects it produces
in the lives of the generality of professing
Christians.   What do they ordinarily
observe there which can lead them to entertain very high ideas of the principles which
give birth to such practices?

Do men of the world discover any
marked, any decided difference between
the conduct of nominal Christians and that
of the rest of their neighbours, who pretend
to no religion at all?   Do they see, in the
daily lives of such, any great abundance of
those fruits by which they have heard believers are to be known?   On the contrary,
do they not discern in them the same
anxious and unwearied pursuit after the

things of earth, as in those who do not profess to have any thought of heaven? Do
not they see them labour as sedulously in
the interests of a debasing and frivolous
dissipation, as those who do not pretend to
have any nobler object in view? Is there
not the same eagerness to plunge into all
sorts of follies themselves, and the same
unrighteous speed in introducing their children to them, as if they had never entered
into a solemn engagement to renounce
them ? Is there not the same self-indul-
gence, the same luxury, and the same pas-
sionate attachment to the things of this
world in *them*, as is visible in those who do
not look for another?

Do not thoughtless neglect, and habitual
carelessness answer, as to society, all the ends
of the most decided infidelity ? Between
the barely decent and the openly profane
there is indeed this difference,—That the
one, by making no profession, deceives
neither the world nor his own heart ; while
the other, by entrenching himself in forms,

fancies that he does something, and thanks God that "he is not like this publican." The one only shuts his eyes upon the danger which the other despises.

But these unfruitful professors would do well to recollect that, by a conduct so little worthy of their high calling, they not only violate themselves the law to which they have vowed obedience, but occasion many to disbelieve or to despise it; that they are thus in a great measure accountable for the infidelity of others, and of course will have to answer for more than their own personal offences. For did they in any respect live up to the principles they profess; did they adorn the doctrines of Christianity by a life in any degree consonant to their faith; did they exhibit any thing of the "beauty of holiness" in their daily conversation; they would then give such a demonstrative proof, not only of the sincerity of their own obedience, but of the brightness of that divine light by which they profess to walk, that the most determined unbeliever would at last begin to think there must be *something* in a religion of which the effects were so visible, and the fruits so amiable; and might in time be led to " glorify," not *them,* not the imperfect doers of these works, but " their Father which is in heaven." Whereas, as things are at present carried on, the obvious conclusion must be, either that Christians do not believe in the religion they profess, or that there is no truth in the religion itself, or that it is of no potency to influence practice.

For, will he not naturally say, that if its influences were so predominant, its consequences *must* be more evident? that if the prize held out were really so bright, those who truly believe so, would surely *do* something, and *sacrifice* something to obtain it ?

This effect of the careless conduct of believers on the hearts of others, will probably be a heavy aggravation of their own guilt at the final reckoning :—and there is no negligent Christian can guess where the infection of his example may stop ; or how remotely it may be pleaded as a palliation of the sins of others, who either may think themselves safe while they are only doing what Christians allow themselves to do ; or who may adduce a Christian's habitual violation of the divine law, as a presumptive evidence that there is no truth in Christianity.

This swells the amount of the actual mischief beyond calculation ; and there is something terrible in the idea of this sort of indefinite evil, that the careless Christian can never know the extent of the contagion which he spreads, nor the multiplied infection which *they* may communicate in *their* turn, whom *his* disorders first corrupted.

And there is this farther aggravation of his offence, that he will not only be answerable for all the positive evils of which his example is the cause ; but for the omission of all the probable good which might have been called forth in others, had *his*

actions been consistent with his profession.
What a strong, what an almost irresistible
conviction, would it carry to the hearts of
unbelievers, if they beheld that characteristic
difference in the manners of Christians,
which their profession gives one a right to
expect,—if they saw that disinterestedness,
that humility, sober-mindedness, temperance, simplicity, and sincerity, which are
the unavoidable fruits of a genuine faith,
and which the Bible has taught them to
expect in every Christian!

But, while a man talks like a saint, and
yet lives like a sinner; while he professes to
believe like an apostle, and yet leads the
life of a sensualist; while he talks of an
ardent faith, and yet exhibits a cold and low
practice; while he boasts himself the disciple of a meek Master, and yet is as much
a slave to his passions as they who acknowledge no such authority; while he appears
the proud professor of an humble religion,
or the intemperate champion of a self-denying religion, or the covetous advocate of a

disinterested religion, such a man brings Christianity into disrepute, confirms those in error who might have been awakened to conviction, strengthens doubt into disbelief, and hardens indifference into contempt.

Even among those of a better qast and a purer principle, the excessive restraints of timidity, caution, and that " fear of man, " which bringeth a snare," confine, and almost stifle the generous spirit of an ardent exertion in the cause of religion. Christianity may pathetically expostulate, that it is not always " an open enemy which dis-" honours her," but her " familiar friend." And, " what dost thou more than others ?" is a question which even the good and worthy should often ask themselves, in order to quicken their zeal; to prevent the total stagnation of unexerted principles, on the one hand; or the danger, on the other, of their being driven down the gulph of ruin by the unresisted and confluent tides of temptation, fashion, and example.

In a very strict and mortified age, of

which a scrupulous severity was the predominant character, precautions against an
excessive zeal might, and doubtless would,
be a wholesome and prudent measure. But
in these times of relaxed principle and frigid
indifference, to see people so vigilantly on
their guard against the imaginary mischiefs
of enthusiasm, while they run headlong
into the real opposite perils of a destructive
·licentiousness, reminds us of the one-eyed
animal in the fable; who, living on the
banks of the ocean, never fancied he could
be destroyed any way but by drowning:
but, while he kept that one eye constantly
fixed on the sea, on which side he con-
cluded all the peril lay, he was devoured by
an enemy on the dry land, from which quar-
ter he never suspected any danger.

Are not the mischiefs of an enthusiastic
piety insisted on with as much earnestness,
as if an extravagant devotion were really the
prevailing propensity? Is not the necessity
of moderation as vehemently urged as if an
intemperate zeal were the epidemic dis-

temper of the great world? as if all our
apparent danger and natural bias lay on the
side of a too rigid austerity, which required
the discreet and constant counteraction of
an opposite principle? Would not a stranger
be almost tempted to imagine, from the frequent invectives against extreme strictness,
that abstraction from the world, and a mo-
nastic rage for retreat, were the ruling temper? that we were in some danger of seeing,
our places of diversion abandoned, and the
enthusiastic scenes of the *Holy Fathers of
the desert* acted over again by the frantic
and uncontrollable devotion of our young
persons of fashion?

It is not to be denied, that enthusiasm is
an evil to which the more religious of the
lower class are peculiarly exposed, and this
from a variety of causes, upon which this
is not the place to enlarge. But who will
be hardy enough to assert, that the class we
are now addressing commonly fall into the
same error? In order to establish the fact, or
to overthrow the assertion, let each fashion-

able reader confess whether, within the sphere
of his own observation, the charge be re-
alized. Let each bring this vague accusation
specifically home to his own acquaintance.
Let him honestly declare what proportion of
noble enthusiasts, what number of honourable fanatics, his own personal knowlege of
the great world supplies him with. Let him
compare the list of his enthusiastic with
that of his luxurious friends, of his fanatical
with his irreligious acquaintance, of "the
" righteous over much" with such as " care
" for none of these things ;" of the strict
and precise with that of the loose and irregular, of those who beggar themselves by
their pious alms with those who injure their
fortune by extravagance ; of those who
" are lovers of God" with those who are
" lovers of pleasure." Let him declare
whether he sees more of his own associates
swallowed up in gloomy meditation or
immersed in sensuality ; whether more are
the slaves of superstitious observances, or of
worldly ambition.

Surely those who address the rich and great in the way of exhortation and reproof, would do particularly well to define exactly what is indeed the prevailing character; lest, for want of such discrimination they should heighten the disease they might wish to cure, and increase the bias they would desire to counteract, by addressing to the voluptuary cautions which belong to the hermit, and thus aggravate his already inflamed appetites by invectives against an evil of which he is in little danger.

If, however, superstition, where it really does exist, injures religion, and we grant that it greatly injures it, yet we insist that scepticism injures it no less : for to deride, or to omit, any of the component parts of Christian faith, is surely not a less fatal evil than making uncommanded additions to it.

Again, if enthusiasm disfigures Christianity, and we grant that it greatly disfigures it, yet surely those who reject Christianity, or who live as if there were

no Christianity in the world, can never
prove themselves to be right, because they
can easily prove enthusiasm to be wrong.

It is seriously to be regretted in an age
like the present, remarkable for indifference
in religion and levity in manners, and which
stands so much in need of lively patterns of
firm and resolute piety, it is I say to be
regretted, that many who really are
Christians on the soberest conviction,
should not appear more openly and decidedly on the side. they have espoused;
that they should assimilate so very much with
the manners of those about them—which
manners they yet scruple not to disap-
prove—and, instead of an avowed but
prudent stedfastness, which might draw
over the others, appear evidently fearful of
being thought precise and over scrupulous;
and actually seem to disavow their right
principles, by concessions and accommo-
dations not strictly consistent with them.
They often seem cautiously afraid of *doing
too much*, and *going too far ;* and the dan-

gerous plea, the necessity of *living like other people*, of *being like the rest of the world*, and the propriety of *not being particular*, is brought as a reasonable apology for a too yielding and indiscriminate conformity.

But, at a time when almost all are sinking into the prevailing corruption, how beautiful a rare, a single integrity is, let the instance of Lot standing out against a whole polluted city, of Noah, resisting the torrent of a whole polluted world declare! And to those with whom a poem is an higher authority than the Bible, let me recommend the most animated picture of a righteous singularity that ever was delineated, in

——The Seraph Abdiel, faithful found
Among the faithless, faithful only he
Among innumerable false, unmov'd,
Unshaken, unseduc'd, unterrify'd,
His loyalty he kept, his love and zeal :
Nor NUMBERS, nor EXAMPLES with him wrought
To swerve from truth, or change his constant mind,
Tho' SINGLE.   PAR. LOST, B. iv.

Few indeed of the more orderly and decent have any objection to that degree of religion which is compatible with their general acceptance with others, or the full enjoyment of their own pleasures. For a formal and ceremonious exercise of the outward duties of Christianity may not only be kept up without exciting censure, but will even procure a certain respect and confidence; and is not quite irreconcileable with a voluptuous and dissipated life. So far many go; and so far as "godliness is " profitable to the life that *is*," it passes not only without reproach, but secures approbation.

" But as soon as men begin to consider religious exercises not as a decency, but an indispensable duty; not as a commutation for a self-denying life, but as a means to promote a holy temper and a virtuous conduct; as soon as they feel disposed to carry the effect of their devotion into their daily life; as soon as their principles discover themselves, by leading them to withdraw from

those scenes, and abstain from those actions
in which the gay place their supreme happiness; as soon as something is to be *done*,
and something is to be *parted with*, then the
world begins to take offence, and to stig-
matize the *activity* of that piety which had
been commended as long as it remained *ino-
perative*, and had only evaporated in *words*.

When religion, like the vital principle,
takes its seat in the heart, and sends out
supplies of life and heat to every part; dif-
fuses motion, spirit, soul, and vigour,
through the whole circulation, and informs
and animates the whole man; when it operates on the practice, influences the conversation, breaks out into a lively zeal for the
honour of God, and the best interests of
mankind,—then the sincerity of heart or
the sanity of mind, of that person will
become questionable; and it must be owing
to a very fortunate combination of circumstances indeed, if he can at once preserve the
character of parts and piety; if he can

retain the reputation of a man of sense after
he has acquired that of a Christian.

  It is surely a folly to talk of being too
holy, too strict, or too good. Where there
really happens to appear some foundation
for the charge of enthusiasm, as there are
indeed sometimes, in good people eccentri-
cities which justify the censure, we may
depend upon it, that it proceeds from some
defect in the judgment, and not from any
excess in the piety: for in goodness there
is no excess: and it is as preposterous to
say that any one is too good, or too pious,
as that he is too wise, too strong, or too
healthy; since the highest point in all these
is only the perfection of that quality which
we admired in a lower degree. There may
be an *imprudent*, but there cannot be a *super-
abundant* goodness. An ardent imagination
may mislead a rightly-turned heart; and a
weak intellect may incline the best inten-
tioned to ascribe too much value to things
of comparatively small importance. Such
a one not having discernment enough to per-

ceive where the force and stress of duty lie, may inadvertently discredit religion by a too scrupulous exactness in points of small intrinsic value. And even well-meaning men as well as hypocrites may think they have done a meritorious service when their " mint" and " anise" are rigorously tithed.

But, in observing the " weightier matters " of the law," in the adoption of the grand peculiarities of the Gospel, in the practice of universal holiness, in the love of God, there can be no possibility of exceeding, while there is no limitation in the command. We, are in no danger of loving our neighbour *better* than ourselves; and let us remember that we do not go beyond, but fall short of the command, while we love him *less*. If we were commanded to love God with *some* of our heart, with *part* of our soul, and a *portion* of our strength, there would then be some colour for those perpetual cavils about the *proportion* of love and the *degree* of obedience which are due to him. But, as the command is so definite, so absolute, so com-

prehensive, so entire, nothing can be more
absurd than that unmeaning, but not unfre-
quent charge, brought against religious
persons, that *they are too strict.* It is in
effect saying, that they love God too much,
and serve him too well; that their hearts are
too intently fixed on heaven, and their
thoughts too sedulously bent on the way to
get thither.

The foundation of this silly censure is
commonly laid in the first principles of education, where an early separation is syste-
matically made between piety and pleasure.
One of the first baits held out for the encouragement of children is, that when they
have done their *duty*, they will be enti-
tled to some *pleasure ;* thus forcibly dis-
joining what should be considered as insé-
parable. And there is not a more common justification of that idle and dissipated
manner in which the second half of the
Sunday is commonly spent, even by those
who make a conscience of spending the
former part properly, than that, " now they

" have done their duty, they may take their
" pleasure."

But while Christian observances are considered as tasks, which are to be got over
to entitle us to something more pleasant;
as a burthen which we must endure in
order to propitiate an inexorable Judge,
who makes a hard bargain with his creatures,
and allows them just so much amusement in
pay for so much drudgery,—we must not
wonder that such low views are entertained
of Christianity, and that a religious life is
reprobated as strict and rigid.

But to him who acts from the nobler
motive of love, and the animating power of
the Christian hope, the exercise is the
reward, the permission is the privilege, the
work is the wages. *He* does not carve out
some miserable pleasure, and stipulate for
some meagre diversion, to pay himself for
the hard performance of his duty, who in
that very performance experiences the highest pleasure; and feels the truest gratification
of which his nature is capable, in devoting

the noblest part of that nature to *His* service, to whom he owes all, because from
Him he has received all.

This reprobated strictness, therefore, so
far from being the source of discomfort
and misery, as is pretended, is in reality the
true cause of actual enjoyment, by laying
the axe to the root of all those turbulent
and uneasy passions, the unreserved and
yet imperfect gratification of which does so
much more tend to disturb our happiness,
than that self-government which Christianity enjoins.

But all precepts seem rigorous, all observances are really hard, where there is not in
the heart an entire conviction of God's right
to our obedience, and an internal principle
of faith and love to make that obedience
pleasant. A religious life is indeed a hard
bondage to one immersed in the practices of
the world, and under the dominion of its
appetites and passions. To a real Christian,
it is " perfect freedom." He does not
now abstain from such and such things,

merely because they are forbidden, as he did in the first stages of his progress, but because his soul has no longer any pleasure in them. And it would be the severest of all punishments to oblige him to return to those practices, from which he once abstained with difficulty, and through the less noble principle of fear.

There is not therefore, perhaps a greater mistake than that common notion entertained by the more orderly part of the fashionable world, that a little religion will make people happy, but that an high degree of it is incompatible with all enjoyment. For surely *that* religion can add little to a man's happiness which restrains him from the commission of a wrong action but which does not pretend to extinguish the bad principle from which the act proceeded. A religion which ties the hands, without changing the heart; which, like the hell of Tantalus, subdues not the desire yet forbids the gratification, is indeed a most uncomfortable religion : and such a

religion, though it may gain a man something on the side of reputation, will give
him but little inward comfort. For what
true peace can that heart enjoy which is
left a prey to that temper which produced
the evil, even though terror or shame may
have prevented the outward act.

That people devoted to the pursuits of a
vain and voluptuous life, should conceive of
religion as a difficult and even unattainable
state, it is easy to believe. That they
should conceive of it as an unhappy state,
is the consummation of their error
and their ignorance: for that a *rational*
being should have his understanding
enlightened; that an *immortal* being
should have his views extended and
enlarged : that a *helpless* being should have
the consciousness of assistance, a *sinful* being
the prospect of pardon, or a *fallen* one the
assurance of restoration, does not seem a
probable ground of unhappiness : and on
any other subject but religion such reasoning would not be admissible.

CHAPTER. VI.

A Stranger, from observing the fashionable Mode of Life, would not take this to be a Christian Country.—Lives of Professing Christians examined, by a Comparison with the Gospel.—Christianity not made the Rule of Life, even by those who profess to receive it as an Object of Faith.—Temporizing Writers contribute to lower the Credit of Christianity.—Loose Harangues on Morals not caculated to ·reform the Heart.

THE Christian religion is not intended, as some of its fashionable professors seem to fancy, to operate as a charm, a talisman, or incantation, and to produce its effect by our pronouncing certain mystical words, attending at certain consecrated places, and performing certain hallowed ceremonies; but it is an active, vital, influential prin-

ciple, operating on the heart, restraining the
desires, affecting the general conduct, and
as much regulating our commerce with the
world, our business, pleasures, and enjoyments, our conversations, designs, and actions, as our behaviour in public worship,
or even in private devotion.

That the effects of such a principle are
strikingly visible in the lives and manners
of the generality of those who give the law
to fashion, will not perhaps be insisted on.
And indeed the whole present system of
fashionable life is utterly destructive of
seriousness. To instance only in the growing habit of frequenting great assemblies,
which is generally thought insignificant, and
is in effect so vapid, that one almost wonders
how it can be dangerous ;—it would excite
laughter, because we are so broken into the
habit, where I to insist on the immorality of
passing one's whole life in a crowd.—But
those promiscuous myriads which compose
the society, falsely so called, of the gay
world ; who are brought together without

esteem, remain without pleasure, and part
without regret; who live in a round of diversions, the possession of which is so joyless,
though the absence is so insupportable;
these, by the mere force of incessant and indiscriminate association, weaken, and in
time wear out, the best feelings and affections of the human heart. And the
mere spirit of dissipation, thus contracted
from invariable habit, even detached from
all its concomitant evils is in itself as hostile
to a religious spirit as more positive and
actual offences. Far be it from me to say
that it is as criminal; I only insist that it is
as opposite to that heavenly-mindedness
which is the essence of the Christian temper.

Let us suppose an ignorant and unpreju-
diced spectator, who should have been
taught the theory of all the religions
on the globe, brought hither from the
other hemisphere. Set him down in the
politest part of our capital, and let him
determine, if he can, except from what he
shall seem interwoven in the texture of our

laws, and kept up in the service of our churches, to what particular religion we belong. Let him not mix entirely with the most flagitious, but only with the most fashionable ; at least, let him keep what they themselves call *the best company.* Let him scrutinize into the manners, customs, conversations, habits, and diversions, most in vogue, and then infer from all he has seen and heard, what is the established religion of the land.

That it could not be the Jewish he would soon discover ; for of rites, ceremonies, and external observances, he would trace but slender remains. He would be equally convinced that it could not be the religion of 'Old Greece and Rome ; for that enjoined reverence to the gods, and inculcated obedience to the laws. His most probable conclusion would be in favour of the Mahometan faith, did not the excessive indulgence of some of the most distinguished, in an article of intemperance prohibited even by

the sensual Prophet of Arabia, defeat that
conjecture.

How will the petrified inquirer be
astonished, if he were told that all these
gay, thoughtless, luxurious, dissipated persons, professed a religion meek, spiritual,
self-denying; of which humility, poverty
of spirit, a renewed mind, and noncon-
formity to the world, were specific distinctions !

When he saw the sons of men of fortune,
scarcely old enough to be sent to school,
admitted to be spectators of the turbulent
and unnatural diversions of racing and
gaming; and the almost infant-daughters,
even of wise and virtuous mothers (an innovation which fashion herself forbade till
now) carried with most unthrifty antici-
pation to the frequent and late protracted
ball,—would he believe that we were of a
religion which has required from these very
parents, a solemn vow that these children
should be bred up "in the nurture and ad-
"monition of the Lord?" That they

should constantly " believe God's holy
" word, and keep his commandments?".

When he observed the turmoils of ambition, the competitions of vanity, the
ardent thirst for the possession of wealth,
and the wild misapplication of it when
possessed; how could he persuade himself
that all these anxious pursuers of present
enjoyment were the disciples of a Master
who exhibited the very character and
essence of his religion, as it were in a
motto—" My Kingdom is not of this
World?"

When he beheld those nocturnal clubs,
so subversive of private virtue and domestic
happiness, would he conceive that we
were of a religion which in express terms
." exhorts young men to be sober-minded?"

When he saw those magnificent and
brightly-illuminated structures which decorate and disgrace the very precincts of
the royal residence (to free itself from all
these pollutions;) when he beheld the
nightly offerings made to the demon of

play on whose cruel altar the fortune and happiness of wives and children are offered up without remorse; would he not conclude that we were of some of those barbarous religions which enjoin unnatural sacrifices, and whose horrid deities are appeased with nothing less than human victims?

Now ought we not to pardon our imaginary spectator, if he should not at once conclude that all the various descriptions of persons above noticed professed the Christian religion; supposing him to have no other way of determining but by the conformity of their manners to that rule by which he had undertaken to judge them? We indeed ourselves must judge with a certain latitude, and candidly take the present state of society into the account; which, in some few instances perhaps, must be allowed to dispense with that literal strictness, which more peculiarly belonged to the first ages of the Gospel.

But as this is really a Christian country,

professing to enjoy the purest faith in the
purest form, it cannot be unreasonable to
go a little farther, and inquire whether
Christianity, however firmly established
and generally professed in it, is really practised by that order of fashionable persons,
who, while they are absorbed in the delights of the world, and their whole souls
devoted to the pursuit of pleasure, yet still
arrogate to themselves the honourable
name of Christians, and occasionally
testify their claim to this high character,
by a general profession of their belief in,
and a decent occasional compliance with
the forms of religion, and the ordinances
of our church ?

This inquiry must be made, not by a
comparison with the state of Christianity
in other countries ; (a mode always fallacious whether adopted by nations or individuals is that of comparing themselves
with those who are still worse;) nor must
it be made from any notions drawn from
custom, decency, or any other human

standard ; but from a scripture view of
what real religion is ;—from any one of
those striking and comprehensive representations of it which may be found con-
densed in so many single passages of the
sacred writings.

Whoever then looks into the Book of
God, and observes its prevailing spirit, and
then looks into that part of the world
under consideration, will not surely be
thought very censorious, if he pronounce
that the conformity between them does not
seem to be *very* striking; and that the
manners of the one do not very evidently
appear to be dictated by the spirit of the
other. Will he discover that the Christian
religion is so much as pretended to be made
the *rule of life* even by that decent order
who profess not to have discarded it as an
object of faith? Do even the more regular,
who neglect not public observances, consider Christianity as *the measure of their
actions?* Do even what the world calls
religious persons employ their time, their

abilities, ánd their fortune, as talents
for which they however confess they
believe themselves accountable; or do they
in any respect live, I will not say up to their
profession (for what human being does so?)
but in any consistency with it, or even with
an eye to its predominant tendencies?
Do persons in general of this description
seem to consider the peculiar doctrines of
the Gospel as any thing more than a form
of words, necessary indeed to be repeated,
and proper to be believed? But do they
consider them as necessary to be adopted
into a governing principle of action?

Is it acting a consistent part to declare in
the solemn assemblies that they are " miser-
" able offenders," and that " there is no
" health in them," and yet never in their
daily lives to discover any symptom of that
humility and self-abasement, which should
naturally be implied in such a declaration?

Is it reasonable or compatible, I will not
say with piety, but with good sense, earnestly
to lament having " followed the devices and

" desires of their own hearts," and then deliberately to plunge into such a torrent of dissipations as clearly indicates that they do not struggle to oppose *one* of these devices, to resist *one* of these desires? I dare not say this is hypocrisy, I do not believe it is, but surely it is inconsistency.

" Be ye not conformed to this world," is a leading principle in the book they acknowledge as their guide. But after unresistingly assenting to this as a doctrinal truth, at church,—how absurd would they think any one who should expect them to adopt it into their practice! Perhaps the whole law of God does not exhibit a single precept more expressly, more steadily, and more uniformly rejected by the class in question. If it mean any thing, it can hardly be consistent with that mode of life emphatically distinguished by the appellation of *fashionable.*

Now, would it be much more absurd (for any other reason but because it is not the custom) if our legislators were to meet

one day in every week, gravely to read
over all the obsolete statutes and rescinded
acts of parliament, than it is for the order
of persons of the above description to as-
semble every Sunday, to profess their belief
in and submission to a system of principles
which they do not so much as *intend* shall
be binding on their practice ?

, But to continue our inquiry.— There is
not a more common or more intelligible definition of human duty, than that of " Fear
" God, and keep his commandments."
Now, as to the first of these inseparable
precepts, can we, with the utmost stretch
of charity, be very forward to conclude
that God is really " very greatly feared,"
in secret, by those who give too manifest
indications that they live " without him in
" the world ?" And as to the latter precept, which naturally grows out of the
other—without noticing any of the flagrant
breaches of the moral law, let us only confine ourselves to the allowed, general, and
notorious violation of the third and fourth

commandments, by the higher as well as by
the lower orders ; breaches so flagrant, that
they force themselves on the observation of
the most inattentive, too palpably to be
either unnoticed or palliated.

Shall we have reason to change our
opinion if we take that divine representation
of the sum and substance of religion, and
apply it as a touchstone in the present
trial,—" Thou shalt love the Lord thy God
" with *all* thy heart, and with *all* thy mind,
" and with *all* thy soul, and with *all* thy
" strength, and thy neighbour as thyself ?"
Now, judging by inference, do we see
many public proofs of that heavenly-mindedness which would be the inevitable effect
of such a fervent and animated dedication
of all the powers, faculties, and affections
of the soul to him who gave it? And, as
to the great rule of social duty expressed in
the second clause, do we observe as much
of that considerate kindness, that pure disinterestedness, that conscientious attention to
the comfort of others, especially of depend-

ents and inferiors, as might be expected
from those who enjoy the privilege of so
unerring a standard of conduct? a standard
which, if impartially consulted, must make
our kindness to others bear an exact proportion to our self-love: a rule in which
Christian principle, operating on human
sensibility, could not fail to decide aright
in every supposable case. For no man can
doubt how he ought to act towards another,
while the inward-corresponding suggestions
of conscience and feeling concur in letting
him know how he would wish, in a change
of circumstances, that others should act
towards him.

Or suppose we take a more detailed sur-
vey, by a third rule, which indeed is not
so much the principle as the effect of piety—
" True religion, and undefiled, before God
" and the Father, is this: to visit the
" fatherless and widows in their affliction;
" and to keep himself *unspotted from the*
" *world.*" Now, if Christianity insists that
obedience to the latter injunction be the

true evidence of the sincerity of those who fulfil the former, is the beneficence of the fashionable world *very* strikingly illustrated by this spotless purity, this exemption from the pollutions of the world, which is here declared to be its invariable concomitant?

But if we were to venture to take our estimate with a view more immediately evangelical; if we presumed to look for that genuine Christianity which consists in " repentance towards God, and faith in our " Lord Jesus Christ;" to insist that, whatever *natural* religion and *fashionable* religion may teach, it is the peculiarity of the *Christian* religion to humble the sinner and exalt the Saviour; to insist that not only the grossly flagitious, but that *all* have sinned; that *all* are by nature in a state of condemnation? that *all* stand in need of mercy, of which there is no hope but on the Gospel terms; that eternal life is promised to those *only* who accept it on the offered conditions of " faith, repentance, and renewed obedience;"—if we were to insist on such evidences of our Christianity as these; if we were to express these doctrines in plain scriptural terms, without lowering, qualifying, disguising, or doing them away; if we were to insist on this belief, and its implied and corresponding practices! we are aware that, with whatever condescending patience this little tract might have been so far perused, many a fashionable reader would here throw it aside, as having now detected the palpable enthusiast, the abettor of " strange doctrines," long ago consigned over by the liberal and the polite to bigots and fanatics. And yet, if the Bible be true, this is a simple and faithful description of Christianity.

Surely, men forget that we are urging them upon their own principles; that while we are pressing them with motives drawn from Christianity, they seem to have as little concern in those motives as if they themselves were of another religion. It is not a name that will stand us in stead. It is not merely glorying in the title of

Christians, while we are living in the neglect of its precepts; it is not valuing ourselves on the profession of religion as creditable, while we reject the power of it as fanatical, that will save us. In any other circumstance of life it would be accounted absurd to have a set of propositions, principles, statutes, or fundamental articles, and not to make them the ground of our acting as well as of our reasoning. In these supposed instances the blame would lie in the contradiction; in religion it lies in the agreement. Strange! that to act in consequence of received and acknowledged principles, should be accounted weakness! Strange, that what alone is truly consistent, should be branded as absurd! Strange that men must really forbear to act rationally, only that they may not be reckoned mad! Strange, that they should be commended for having prayed in the excellent words of the Bible and of our church, for " a clean " heart, and a right spirit;" and yet, if they gave any sign of such a transfor-

mation of heart, they should be accounted,
if not fantastical, at least, singular, weak,
or melancholy men.

After having, however, just ventured to
hint at what are indeed the humbling
doctrines of the gospel, the doctrines to
which alone eternal life is promised, we
shall in deep humility forbear to enlarge
on this part of the subject, which has been
exhausted by the labours of wise and pious
men in all ages. Unhappily, however, the
most awakening of these writers are not
the favourite guests in the closets of the
more fashionable Christians ; who, when
they happen to be more seriously disposed
than ordinary, are fond of finding out
some middle kind of reading, which re-
commends some half-way state, something
between Paganism and Christianity, sus-
pending the mind, like the position of
Mahomet's tomb, between earth and
heaven :—a kind of reading which,
while it quiets the conscience by being on
the side of morals, neither awakens fear,

nor alarms security. By dealing in generals, it comes home to the hearts of none :
it flatters the passions of the reader, by
ascribing high merit to the performance of
certain right actions, and the forbearance
from certain wrong ones ; among which,
that reader must be very unlucky indeed
who does not find some performances and
some forbearances of his own. It at once
enables him to keep heaven in his eye, and
the world in his heart. It agreeably repre-
sents the readers to themselves as amiable
persons, guilty indeed of a few faults, but
never as condemned sinners under sentence
of death. It commonly abounds with high
encomiums on the dignity of human nature;
the good effects of virtue and health, fortune, and reputation ; the dangers of a
blind zeal, the mischiefs of enthusiasm, and
the folly of singularity, with various other
kindred sentiments ; which, if they do not
fall in of themselves with the corruptions
of our nature, may, by a little warping, be
easily accommodated to them.

These are the too successful practices of certain lukewarm and temporising writers, who have become popular by blunting the edge of that heavenly-tempered weapon, whose salutary keenness, but for their " de-" ceitful handling," would oftener "pierce to " the dividing asunder of soul and spirit."

But those severer preachers of righteousness, who disgust by applying too closely to the conscience; who probe the inmost heart, and lay open all its latent peccancies ; who treat of principles as the only certain source of manners ; who lay the axe to the root, oftener than the pruning knife to the branch ; who insist much and often on the great leading truths, that man is a fallen creature; who must be restored, if he be restored at all, by means very little flattering to human pride,—such heart-searching writers as these will seldom find access to the houses and hearts of the more modish Christians, unless they happen to owe their admission to some subordinate quality of style ; unless they can captivate, with the seducing graces of language, those well-bred readers, who are childishly amusing themselves with the garnish, when they are perishing for want of food ; who are searching for polished periods when they should be in quest of alarming truths; who are looking for elegance of composition when they should be anxious for eternal life.

' Whatever comparative praise may be due to the former class of writers, when viewed with others of a less decent order, yet I am not sure whether so many books of frigid morality, exhibiting such inferior motives of action, such moderate representations of duty, and such a low standard of principle, have not done religion much more harm than good; whether they do not lead many a reader to inquire what is the lowest degree in the scale of virtue with which he may content himself, so as barely to escape eternal punishment; how much indulgence he may allow himself, without absolutely forfeiting his chance of safety : what is the uttermost verge to which he

may venture of this world's enjoyment,
and yet just keep within a possibility of
hope for the next : adjusting the scales of
indulgence and security with such a scrupulous equilibrium, as not to lose much pleasure, yet not incur much penalty.

This is hardly an exaggerated representation : and to these low views of duty
is partly owing so much of that bare-weight
virtue with which even Christians are so
apt to content themselves : fighting for
every inch of ground which may possibly be
taken within the pales of permission, and
stretching those pales to the utmost edge of
that limitation about which the world and
the Bible contend.

But while the nominal Christian is per-
suading himself that there can be no harm
in going *a little farther*, the real Christian
is always afraid of going too far. While
the one is debating for a little more disputed
ground, the other is so fearful of straying
into the regions of unallowed indulgence,
that he keeps at a prudent distance from

the extremity of his permitted limits; and
is as anxious in restricting as the other is
desirous of extending them. One thing is
clear, and it may be no bad indication by
which to discover the state of a man's heart
to himself; while he is contending for
this allowance, and stipulating for the
other indulgence, it will shew him that,
whatever change there may be in his life,
there is none in his heart; the temper remains as it did; and it is by the inward
frame rather than the outward act that he
can best judge of his *own* state, whatever
may be the rule by which he undertakes
to judge of that of another.

It is less wonderful that there are not
more Christians, than that Christians, as
they are called, are not better men; for if
Christianity be not true, the motives to
virtue are not high enough to quicken ordinary men to very extraordinary exertions.
We see them do and suffer every day for
popularity, for custom, for fashion, for the
point of honour, not only more than good

men do and suffer for religion, but a great
deal more than religion requires them to do.
For her *reasonable service* demands no
sacrifices but what are sanctioned by good
sense, sound policy, right reason, and uncorrupt judgment.

Many of these fashionable professors
even go so far as to bring their right faith
as an apology for their wrong practice.
They have a commodious way of intrenching themselves within the shelter of some
general position of unquestionable truth:
Even the great Christian hope becomes a
snare to them. They apologize for a life
of offence by taking refuge in the supreme
goodness they are abusing. That "God is
"all merciful," is the common reply to
those who hint to them their danger.
This is a false and fatal application of a
divine and comfortable truth. Nothing
can be more certain than the proposition,
nor more delusive than the inference: for
their deduction implies, not that he is
merciful to sin repented of, but to sin continued in. But it is a most fallacious

hope to expect that God will violate his own covenant, or that he is indeed, " all mercy," to the utter exclusion of his other attributes of perfect holiness, purity, and justice.

It is a dangerous folly to rest on these vague and general notions of indefinite mercy; and nothing can be more delusive than this indefinite trust in being forgiven in our *own* way, after God has clearly revealed to us that he will only forgive us in *his* way. Besides, is there not something singularly base in sinning against God *because* he is merciful ?

But the truth is, no one does truly trust in God, who does not endeavour to obey him. For to break his laws, and yet to depend on his favour ; to live in opposition to his will, and yet in expectation of his mercy ; to violate his commands, and yet look for his acceptance, would not, in any other instance, be thought a reasonable ground of conduct ; and yet it is by no means as uncommon as it is inconsistent.

CHAPTER. VII.

View of those who acknowledge Christianity as a perfect System of Morals, but deny its Divine Authority. — Morality not the Whole of Religion.

As in the preceding chapter notice was taken of that description of persons who profess to receive Christianity with great reverence as a matter of faith, who yet do not pretend to adopt it as a rule of conduct; I shall conclude these slight remarks with some short animadversions on another set of men, and that not a small one, among the decent and the fashionable, who profess to think it exhibits an admirable system of morals, while they deny its divine authority; though that authority alone can make the necessity of obeying its precepts binding on the consciences of men.

This is a very discreet scheme : for such persons at once save themselves from the discredit of having their understanding imposed upon by a supposed blind submission to evidences and authorities ; and yet, prudently enough, secure to themselves, in no small degree, the reputation of good men. By steering this middle kind of course, they contrive to be reckoned liberal by the *philosophers,* and decent by the believers.

But we are not to expect to see the pure morality of the Gospel very carefully transfused into the lives of such objectors. And indeed it would be unjust to imagine that the precepts *should* be most scrupulously observed by those who reject the authority. The influence of divine truth must necessarily best prepare the heart for an unreserved obedience to its laws. If we do not depend on the offers of the Gospel, we shall want the best motive to the actions and and performances which it enjoins. A lively belief *must* therefore precede a hearty obedi-

ence. Let those who think otherwise hear
what the Saviour of the World has said :
" For this end was I born, and for this
" cause came I into the world, that I might
" bear witness unto the truth." Those
who reject the Gospel, therefore, reject the
power of performing good actions. That
command, for instance, to set " our affec-
" tions on things above," will operate but
faintly, till that spirit from which the command proceeds touches the heart, and convinces it that no human good is worthy of
the entire affection of an immortal creature.
An unreserved faith in the promiser *must*
precede our acceptable performance of any
duty to which the promise is annexed.

But as to a set of duties enforced by no
other motive than a bare acquiescence in
their beauty, and a cold conviction of their
propriety, but impelled by no obedience to
his authority who imposes them ; though
we know not how well they might be performed by pure and impeccable beings, yet
we know how they commonly *are* per-

formed by frail and disorderly creatures, fallen from their innocence, and corrupt in their very natures.

Nothing but a conviction of the truth of Christianity can reconcile thinking beings to the extraordinary appearances of things in the, Creator's moral government of the world. The works of God are an enigma, of which his word alone is the solution. The dark veil which is thrown over the divine dispensations in this lower world, must naturally shock those who consider only the single scene which is acting on the present stage; but is reconcileable to him who, having learnt from revelation the nature of the laws by which the great Author acts, trusts confidently that the catastrophe will set all to rights. The confusion which sin and the passions have introduced; the triumph of wickedness; the seemingly arbitrary disproportion of human conditions, accountable on no scheme but that which the Gospel has opened to us—have all a natural tendency to withdraw from the love of God the hearts of those who erect themselves into critics on the divine conduct, and yet will not study the plan, and get acquainted with the rules, so far as it has pleased the Supreme Disposer to reveal them.

Till therefore the word of God is used as "a lamp to their paths," men can neither truly discern the crookedness of their own ways, nor the perfection of that light by which they are directed to walk. And this light can only be seen by its own proper brightness: it has no other medium. Until therefore "the secret of the Lord" is with men they will not truly "fear him;" until he has "enlarged their hearts" with the knowledge and belief of his word, they will not very vigorously run "the way of his "commandments." Until they have acquired that "faith, without which it is im-"possible to please God," they will not attain that "holiness, without which no man can "see him."

And indeed if God has thought fit to

make the Gospel an instrument of salvation,
we must own the necessity of receiving it as
a divine institution, before it is likely to
operate very effectually on the human conduct. The great Creator, if we may judge by
analogy from natural things, is so just and
wise an œconomist, that he always adapts,
with the most accurate precision, the instrument to the work; and never lavishes more
means than are necessary to accomplish the
proposed end. If therefore Christianity had
been intended, for nothing more than a mere
system of ethics, such a system surely might
have been produced at an infinitely less expence. The long chain of prophecy, the
succession of miracles, the labours of apostles, the blood of the saints, to say nothing
of the great and costly sacrifice which the
Gospel records, might surely have been
spared. Lessons of mere human virtue
might have been delivered by some suitable
instrument of human wisdom, strengthened
by the visible authority of human power.
A bare system of morals might have been

communicated to mankind with a more reasonable prospect of advantage, by means not so repugnant to human pride. A mere scheme of conduct might have been delivered with far greater probability of the success of its reception by Antoninus the emperor, or Plato the philosopher, than by Paul the tent-maker, or Peter the fisherman,

Christianity, then, must be embraced entirely, if it be received at all. It must be taken, without mutilation, as a perfect scheme, in the way in which God has been pleased to reveal it. It must be accepted, not as exhibiting beautiful parts, but as presenting one consummate whole, of which the perfection arises from coherence and dependence, from relation and consistency. Its power will be weakened, and its energy destroyed, if every caviller pulls out a pin, or obstructs a spring with the presumptuous view of new modelling the divine work, and making it go to his own mind. There must be no breaking this system into portions of which we are at liberty to choose one and reject another. There is no separating the evidences from the doctrines, the doctrines from the precepts, belief from obedience, morality from piety, the love of our neighbour from the love of God. If we allow Christianity to be any thing, we must allow it to be every thing: if we allow the Divine Author to be indeed unto us " wisdom and righteousness," he must be also " sanctification and redemption."

Christianity then is assuredly something more than a mere set of rules; and faith, though it never pretended to be the substitute for an useful life, is indispensably necessary to its acceptance with God. The Gospel never offers to make religion supercede morality, but every where clearly proves that morality is not the whole of religion. Piety is not only necessary as a *means*, but is itself a most important *end*. It is not only the best principle of moral conduct, but is an indispensable and absolute duty in itself. It is not only the highest motive to the practice of virtue, but is a prior obligation, and absolutely necessary, even when detached from its immediate influence on outward actions. Religion will survive all the virtues of which it is the source; for we shall be living in the noblest exercises of piety when we shall have no objects on which to exercise many human virtues. When there will be no distress to be relieved, no injuries to be forgiven, no evil habits to be, subdued, there will be a Creator to be blessed and adored, a Redeemer to be loved and praised.

To conclude, a real Christian is not such merely by habit, profession, or education; he is not a Christian in order to acquit his sponsors of the engagements they entered into in his name; but he is one who has embraced Christianity from a conviction of its truth, and an experience of its excellence. He is not only confident in matters of faith by evidences suggested to his understanding, or reasons which correspond to his enquiries; but all these evidences of

truth, all these principles of goodness, are
worked into his heart, and exhibit themselves in his practice. He sees so much of
the body of the great truths and fundamental
points of religion, that he has a satisfactory
trust in those lesser branches which ramify
to infinity from the parent stock ; though
he may not individually and completely
comprehend them all. He is so powerfully
convinced of the general truth, and so
deeply impressed by the general spirit of the
Gospel, that he is not startled by every
little difficulty, he is not staggered by every
" hard saying." Those depths of mystery
which surpass his understanding do not
shake his faith, and this, not because he is
credulous, and given to take things upon
trust, but because, knowing that his founda-
tions are right, he sees how one truth of
scripture supports another like the bearings
of a geometrical building ; because he sees
the aspect one doctrine has upon another ;
because he sees the consistency of each with
the rest, and the place, order, and relation

of all. The real Christian by no means rejects reason from his religion; so far from it, he most carefully exercises it in furnishing his mind with all the proofs and evidences of its truth. But he does not stop here. Christianity furnishes him with a living principle of action, with the vital influences of the holy spirit, which, while it enlightens his faculties, rectifies his will, turns his knowledge into practice, sanctifies his heart, changes his habits, and proves, that when faithfully received, the word of truth " is life indeed, and is spirit " indeed!"

THE END.

G. SIDNEY, Printer,
Northumberland Street, Strand.

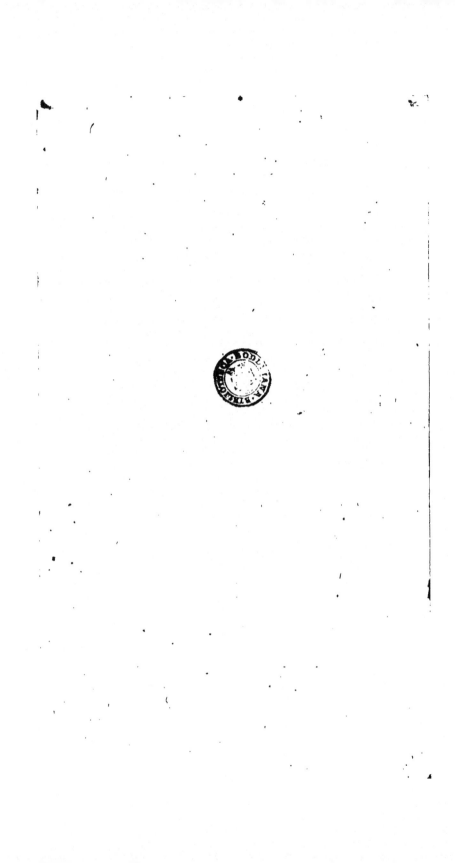

CPSIA information can be obtained at www.ICGtesting.com
Printed in the USA
BVOW06s0556101115

426492BV00013B/100/P